Shadows *and* Silhouettes

Reflections *on* Life's Adventures

Delores Wardell

Author of *Naomi's Place*

For Fiona,

*An angel gifted with intuitive wisdom
and skillful healing hands.*

Contents

Author's Note

ALL INCIDENTS AND DIALOGUE in this book are described to the best of my recollection, although none of my recollections are perfect. The experiences I share are based on real events. I hope to be excused for occasionally yielding to poetic license. I cannot sacrifice a good story for strict exactitude. All the names are fictional, and any similarities between these fictional names and real people is strictly coincidental.

Preface

WHEN THE WORLD WAR against an invisible enemy began, I was traveling in Mexico. Stay-at-home orders came from health officials, but I made it back to the United States just under the wire before the borders were closed and airlines canceled hundreds of flights. COVID-19 became a force that swept across the globe, altering almost everyone's life. It certainly did mine.

For the past seven years I'd been on a mission to remove from my dream list every country I'd ever wanted to visit. I was hardly home, arriving only to prepare for the next adventure. Life was a thrilling whirlwind as I danced in countries on the continents of Europe, South America, Africa, and Asia. Besides travel, my life included ballroom dancing, acting classes, theater productions, lectures on Fridays at the local community college, and Sunday mornings on the golf course. Then as swift and unexpected as a lightning bolt, the war stopped me in my tracks. Life became surreal. Streets emptied, restaurants folded, future trips were canceled, and daily reports brought news of staggering numbers of those who had not survived the war.

For the first few months when the world was in quarantine, I busied myself with projects that had been on hold. I cleaned out closets, organized drawers, sorted through files that needed shredding, rearranged the garage, donated shelves of items to thrift stores, worked on jigsaw puzzles, became reacquainted with old music scores—and then I ran out of ideas for keeping busy.

Within this great pause, I found contemplative time to look back on my life. Many memories of happiness and sorrow edged me toward my computer. I began to gather them into stories: some I'd started in the past and put aside, and others emerged as I read old scripts. This, dear reader, is how I finally battled COVID-19 and won against ennui, a potentially lethal side effect of the coronavirus.

The stories I selected are broken into three periods of my life: work, travel, and reflection. Part I deals with the people and experiences I encountered in my work as a clinical psychologist in the juvenile court system or in my private practice.

As part of my internship, I spent three thousand hours of supervised training in the juvenile court system. After passing the board exams to become a licensed psychologist, I stayed at the court for several more years. The team was a multidiscipline unit made up of psychologists, social workers, a nurse, and a psychiatrist. My job included evaluating families who entered the system and providing counseling services to children who had been removed from their families, as well as to offenders who were serving their sentences in a long-term facility or Juvenile Hall.

Juvenile Hall can be an overwhelming place at first. A large metal door clangs shut after it is opened by an electrical device. Once inside you are hit by the smells of urine and body odor and the sounds of panicky youth screaming objections to incarceration or staff yelling for help with an out-of-control youngster. Our team was close-knit because like combat soldiers, we guarded each other's emotional backs. In weekly staff meetings we shared our encounters with clients we evaluated. Two of the stories herein, "The Sisters" and "Fire and Chess" were told by two different doctors in these meetings; I've taken the liberty to write their experiences in my own words. The purpose is to provide a panoply of our daily life on the job.

The Hall was a vibrant place filled with public defenders, probation officers, district attorneys, chaplains, and social workers, who all took great pride in trying to turn around troubled youth. Before the days of reality shows, we used to say that someone could roll a camera into our setting and, without editing, viewers could witness stories that would make them think they were on a film set where tales of fiction are woven. Wasn't it Mark Twain that penned something about truth being stranger than fiction?

When I left my job at the juvenile court, I entered the calmer world of private practice. Unlike in the court where scant hope hung by a frayed, worn thread, people came to my practice full of optimism, hoping for miracles. After thirty years in private practice, I ended my career in the conservator's office, coming full circle to find myself back in court as an evaluator on behalf of those who were unable to manage their affairs.

Stories in part II are about trips I took in my young adult years. Reviewing old journals, I selected a few that brought a smile to my lips and struck fear in my heart. What was I thinking? Older and wiser, today I most likely would not take the risks or face the challenges that I did when I was younger. I added a story that my husband had written about stealing our boat. I wanted to include it as it closed another chapter of my life.

And finally, part III includes my reflections about events that either puzzled me or brought me to an awareness of myself in a new way.

How does one select a story from so vast a store of memories? It's like tossing confetti in the air and randomly plucking pieces that catch the eye. For to a writer, every ordinary event holds the promise of being turned into a story. Just yesterday a neighbor told me about friends who had been stranded overseas due to COVID-19. After listening to the fascinating details, I exclaimed, "You must write about it. It belongs in the archive of COVID stories." She looked back at me with a blank stare. See what I mean about a writer smelling a good story?

I invite you to read the stories of mundane events and chance happenings. I do not claim that my life has been more unique or exceptional than yours or that I was braver or wiser than you. But I believe that through our shared stories our commonality is revealed. These stories reflect only shadows of places and silhouettes of persons who passed through my life and touched me in some manner. My hope is that they will inspire you to pen your own adventures.

PART I

Work

O, how full of briers
is this working-day world!
—WILLIAM SHAKESPEARE, *AS YOU LIKE IT*

CHAPTER 1

First Day

"DON'T MOVE OR I'LL shoot," screamed the boy who swung a gun wildly, waving it as though it were no more than a garden hose and he was watering flowers. At the same time, he backed up against the cafeteria doors to prevent anyone from entering.

I caught a glimpse of him before ducking beneath a table. Crouching behind Dr. Gary McLeod, shielded by his large frame, I peered around him to get another look. I couldn't be sure of the boy's age because of his scrawny, slight build—maybe fifteen, or he could be younger. When he spoke, his voice broke, which didn't sound very commanding, but a gun is all that's needed to keep a room full of strangers obedient. And nothing is more dangerous than a scared boy with a gun.

Ohmigod—my first day on the job and I'm going to be killed. My body trembled, and the blood pounded in my head. The boy's adrenaline seemed about as pumped as mine. He hopped from one foot to the other, wheeling in the direction of any movement. He was the only person in motion; everyone else in the room was frozen as if someone had pushed the pause button on a TV remote.

"You," he said as he pointed the gun at a Hispanic man holding a tray of food. He, too, was caught in a still frame, having just left the food line. The cafeteria had a mix of professionals, employees of the court, and individuals who were waiting for their hearing in front of a judge.

"Mi?" the frightened man asked, pulling the tray into his chest as though to steady himself and the coffee, which threatened to spill out of the cup.

"Yes, you," the boy snapped. "Over here and stand by the door. Tell anyone who tries to come in that this place is closed. *Off limits!* And if you let anyone in, I'll put a bullet in your head. Comprende?"

The man shook his head and in a pleading voice said, "No hablo inglés."

"Jesus Christ, I ought to just shoot you." Every word indicated he was on the verge of panic. Then he turned to the woman behind the frozen Hispanic man and asked with sarcasm, "Do you speak English?"

I caught my breath. Kelly, our unit's nurse, stepped forward. Only ten minutes earlier she had been introduced to me as "the Princess" by our boss Dr. Albert Hastings. It was a fitting name for sure. Kelly could have been the model for Goldilocks or Cinderella or any other fair heroine in a fairy tale. People could be misled by her soft golden curls and heart-shaped face, unless they studied her eyes—eyes mischievous and irreverent. She flashed a smile that seemed to mock whomever she addressed. She smiled at the boy and gave a flippant "Sure, whatever you say."

Her tone appeared to throw him for a moment. Then he drew back and gave her a threatening look, which didn't seem to faze her.

"I know you. You work for that devil Dr. Hastings. That's who I've come to see." He spotted Dr. Hastings sitting at the table farthest from the entry. A few of us who had been sitting with him were still huddled under the table. "Dr. Hastings, I've come for you. I'm going to kill you."

Dr. Hastings tapped his foot nervously, just a few inches away from my ear. He had not left his seat. A few minutes earlier he had been conducting his daily informal staff meeting. He saw it as a time for his staff to socialize and relax before they disappeared inside their offices to face stories that could break one's heart.

I looked up, trying to catch a glimpse of his face. Dr. Hastings, the psychiatrist heading the psychology team that I had just joined, had just been joking with his staff. His calm presence and familiarity with his staff left me with a feeling of camaraderie and well-being—but it was a false sense of safety, I was learning. Now, in the next few minutes, he might be dead.

Dr. Hastings pushed back his chair and stood. His voice was a notch higher than normal when he spoke to the young man.

"Don't do this, Brian. You'll upset everyone. Let's go outside, and you can tell me why you're so angry with me."

Brian had started to move toward Dr. Hastings when he heard Kelly tell someone outside the door, "Sorry, it's closed. For cleaning."

He apparently didn't like her mocking tone of voice, so he screamed at the person trying to get in, "Get the fuck away from the door. Now." He then ordered Kelly, "You tell people who try to come in that we're closed and say it like you mean it. If anyone gets in, they die, and you die."

Kelly gave him a smile, totally unrattled. I'd have wet my pants. The cool that both Kelly and Dr. Hastings showed began to steady me. *They must know how to handle him*, I thought, trying to reassure myself. I edged closer to Dr. McLeod, who was crouched beside me. He turned and gave me a wink as if to assure me not to be afraid. I felt I'd been plopped into a scene from *Alice in Wonderland*. I almost laughed, a gallows laugh, remembering Alice's conversation with the Cheshire Cat. He told Alice to visit the Hatter and the March Hare, warning her that they were both mad.

> "But I don't want to go among mad people," Alice remarked.
> "Oh, you can't help that," said the Cat: "we're all mad here. I'm mad. You're mad."
> "How do you know I'm mad? said Alice.
> "You must be," said the Cat, "or you wouldn't have come here."

Oh, the wisdom that lies within fairy tales.

Brian turned back to Dr. Hastings. "You think you are God. Well, you're not. You can't just go around playing with people's lives. You think you can. But you can't. Now, I'm God. See, I'm the one who says what the future's going to be." His shaky words rang loud in the cavernous room as he spit them.

"Brian, I don't know what you're talking about," Dr. Hastings said calmly.

"Oh, yes, you do. You know damn well. I read your report. You don't think I can live on my own. You think I need to stay in that goddamn group home, like I'm a retard or something.

You said I don't have the maturity to live without supervision. Well, how about this for maturity?" He lifted the gun, pointing it up and down as though it were a scolding finger.

Someone in the room sniggered, seeing the irony of it. Brian screamed, "Who did that? Made that sound? Who laughed? You think this is funny? You won't think it's funny when I'm finished here."

His eyes were searching the room. I looked at the floor. Never, never make eye contact with a lunatic. You never know what he'll see when his eyes connect with yours.

Dr. Hastings seemed to know this kid well, and he seemed to be offering Brian a chance not to mess up his whole life. He talked fast but spoke with a sure, calm voice.

"I do want you to live on your own. I don't expect you to stay a child. I want to see you make it on your own, Brian. I don't feel you are ready for emancipation just yet. You'll get there—in time. Let's go upstairs to my office. Let's talk about this. If you don't like your group home, we'll see about finding another one, one more suitable to your wants. I can't talk to you with a gun in my face; it's too nerve-racking."

"Nerve-racking? You think this is nerve-racking? Well, now you know how it feels, Dr. Hastings, when someone holds a gun on your life? Huh?" Brian was near tears.

"It feels awful. Let's talk, Brian. I'll talk to you upstairs. We'll call your social worker right away and see if we can't find a compromise."

Just as Brian was considering Dr. Hastings's words, there was a commotion at the door. Kelly was talking to a person behind it. Everyone was staring at the door and straining to hear what was being said. Someone was pushing hard against Kelly, determined to get in. In one brief backward step, Kelly was beside Brian just as a large male bolted through the door. It was a bailiff. Brian raised the gun to shoot, but Kelly came up under his arm, hard and swift, forcing Brian's arm upward, and the gun flew out of his hand and landed with a loud crack on the tiled floor. The bailiff tackled Brian, throwing him facedown, and then placed cuffs on him.

Just like that it was over. Kelly walked nonchalantly back toward the table and flashed a little smirk to the staff sitting there. Dr. Hastings slumped to the chair but then leaped to his feet, moving toward the bailiff and Brian. Brian lay on the floor with his arms restrained behind him and the bailiff's knee on the middle of Brian's back. With a swift synchronized movement, the bailiff was on his radio calling for backup. Brian looked up at Dr. Hastings: all the machismo had melted, leaving a sniveling child.

"I'm not getting out, am I? I'll never know what freedom is like," he whined.

"It's not all it's cracked up to be, Brian. It comes with a lot of responsibility. I'll come over to see you later today."

Brian would be taken to Juvenile Hall, a sprawling complex near the court building. The bailiffs took charge, pushing Dr. Hastings aside, as they went about the business of restoring calm. Soon the confusion was cleared away as though the disturbance had been no more than spilled milk. The cafeteria quickly returned to normal. Voices began to rise and spread across the room, but a crackling tension lingered in the air. Anxious eyes turned in the direction of the table where Dr. Hastings again sat with his staff.

Dr. McLeod was the first to toss Kelly kudos for her quick reaction. "Kelly, you're the girl of the hour. Your 4-9 saved the day."

"I wish I had more of it. My high 3 nearly caused me to pass out," said Julie, a pretty intern sitting across from me.

Kelly's hand shook slightly as she raised the coffee cup to her mouth. "You've got to be one to know one," she laughed.

They were referring to their elevated scores on the Minnesota Multiphasic Personality Inventory, informally called the MMPI. This group talks about their personality profiles as though they were blood pressure readings. I couldn't image their being proud of their pathology. Being a 4-9, a typical profile for psychopaths, bore out Kelly's admission: psychopaths don't exhibit anxiety under stress like normal people. And Julie's elevation on the 3 scale indicated high levels of anxiety.

I turned to Kelly and asked, "Did you know him?"

"Oh, yeah. He's been in the system since before he started school. Moved around so many times, one foster home after another. No one wants him."

"What will happen to him now?"

"He just graduated from being a 300 to a 600 kid."

I knew the classifications Kelly referred to: 300 meant a noncriminal case, such as one under the auspices of social services. The 600 code applied to criminal offenses. As in all organizations, one needed to master a lexicon to belong.

"It happens a lot. Dependency kids passing from one system into another," Kelly offered. "You'll see if you stay around long enough."

Dr. Hastings, who spoke more rapidly than usual, said, "A lot of high functioning people out there have psychopathic tendencies but never get in trouble with the law." He segued to the topic of dangerousness. "They leave it up to us in mental health to diagnose the potential for it, but we're no more accurate than police, courts, or district attorneys." Then he shifted to the influence of genes on behavior. "You learn from dogs that you can't make a golden retriever out of a pit bull and vice versa."

The staff had apparently heard this before, and they began to make excuses to get back to their offices. Only Julie and I remained at the table as Dr. Hastings opined further on the importance of genetic influence.

I asked, "Did you think Brian was dangerous? Do you think he's a psychopath?"

"Oh, no, he's just an unruly boy." I nearly choked. Brian seemed more than just unruly. Dr. Hastings quickly continued, "But he's a pretty angry boy and came by his anger honestly. He's never been into criminal activity before. These kids get desperate, then they get their hands on a gun, and the next thing you know their life is ruined." He rose suddenly, "I've got to see the judge. Get to him first. Get him to understand what happened here. Brian's a kid who was raped by his uncle, entered the social services system at age five, and has been trying to get home ever since. But there is no home, and I certainly didn't want to see him living on the streets. He'd be an easy target."

He turned to me and smiled reassuringly: "It isn't like this every day." Then he told Julie to go with me to our office upstairs, adding, "Have Jean assign her to sit in with someone doing an evaluation so she gets oriented. Then show her around." Then he disappeared.

Julie and I rode the elevator to the second floor. There's a way people talk after they share a near-death experience. You'd think we'd been best friends. We walked down the hallway past the offices of the public defenders, turned down another hallway and passed the district attorney's section, and finally came to a cluster of tiny enclosed offices that were assigned to the psychology team working for the court. As we entered the secretary's office, it was abuzz with talk of the incident in the cafeteria. Kelly was saying, "And when I saw it was Jeff at the door, well, how could I keep him out? I can't even keep him out of my bed." Everyone laughed.

Julie introduced me to Jean, a large-framed woman, younger than me, who clearly ran the show. I could see she was sizing me up as she considered my petite size and judged my carefully chosen attire. Then she looked through a stack of charts on her desk, selected one, and handed it to me. "Here's your case for the day," she said.

"I think Dr. Hastings wants me to sit in with someone first," I offered.

"Well, we've got too many cases facing a deadline. We're short two staff, and the court wants an answer on this one tomorrow. You'll not see the whole family; it's just the mother that you'll be evaluating. It should be a piece of cake for someone who's already familiar with the court system." Jean said it with a smile, but there was bite in the words.

I half expected it. After all, I was married to a well-known doctor in the community who was often an expert witness on criminal offenses. He had evaluated cases here in the juvenile court in the past. I anticipated some might feel I had been selected for this coveted internship out of favoritism and I'd have to face some hazing to establish my reputation.

Julie took me to a large room lined with cabinets full of investigative reports on every person passing through the court. A small section at the end of one of the walls contained a cabinet that held psych testing materials. Julie pulled out a template that outlined the questions the court wanted answered.

I leaned against the wall and read the summary of the case given to me. The father was in jail for attempting to sever his twelve-year-old son's testicles. The explanation he gave the investigating officer was that the son wasn't man enough to pass out antisemitic literature to his classmates. The father wanted to teach his son a lesson, and he had a right to punish his son as he saw fit. A younger female child was also taken into custody and was placed in a psychiatric unit when the officer observed scars on her back and legs. The mother had mental health issues that needed to be assessed.

My legs gave way. "It's only the mother," Jean had said. *For God's sake!* So, this was how my mettle was to be tested.

I introduced myself to a disheveled twenty-six-year-old woman. She had to be only fourteen when her son was born— the son born of a madman. I wondered, *Was she mad before she met him, or had she been hollowed out and slowly filled with his madness?*

It was a straightforward evaluation. The diagnosis was evident: schizophrenia. The recommendation was simple, but the horror was monstrous.

At home that night, I stood in the shower for twenty minutes, scrubbing my body raw. *I can't do this. I can't. Evil is madness. I can't let it touch me. I can't let it get inside me.* My tears fell as hard as the water pouring down on me, cleansing me, washing away the sorrow of the day, leaving me spotless. Leaving me ready for whatever tomorrow would bring.

CHAPTER 2

Some Can, Some Can't

THERE'S NO BEST PLACE to start. Each beginning leads to the same tragic end. So, I might as well begin with the New Year's Eve party.

Julie flung open the French doors off the garden room and stepped onto the softly lit patio, where the party was in full swing. At that moment, a light breeze raised her filmy white gown from around her ankles and gently lifted her waist-length brown hair, making it seem as if she were floating as she moved toward the others. *She's an angel*, I thought. A happy, loud cheer rose from the guests. Julie was beautiful and vibrant, and we all competed to be near her.

"Happy New Year," she greeted Dr. Jim with a light kiss. "Where's the champagne?"

He pointed in the direction of the temporary bar positioned under the avocado tree.

She glided toward the bar. Chet, her husband of three years, lingered by the door. He never felt at ease with us. He believed we didn't accept him because he was a truck driver and we all had PhDs. But that wasn't the reason; the truth was that he was forty-five and Julie was twenty-five and we blamed him for robbing the cradle and then subjecting her to rearing his five rowdy kids. He was a classic redneck and she was a Southern blue blood. How could such a match work?

As she poured champagne into her glass, her laugh resonated as a musical cymbal. The light from the ornamental lanterns fell across her face and I saw a smudge on her cheek. What was it? She always looked flawless. Had she been crying? Or could it be something else?

I wrapped my arm around her waist and whispered, "Julie, come with me to the bathroom. You need to fix your face."

She allowed me to steer her toward the door. *If that man has laid a hand on her, I'll throw the SOB out.* It didn't matter that he was a guest in my house. Chet stepped aside and let us pass as we made our way through the garden room to the bathroom.

The minute the door closed, she gripped the sink and her knees buckled. She slid to the floor and buried her face in her hands. As I put my hand on her shoulder, I felt the trembling from her sobs. She tried to speak, but only plaintive sound came from her throat.

I knew it! I knew it. He's hurt her.

When there were no more tears, she rose, bathed her face, turned to me and with a flat voice said, "My mother died tonight."

Before I could gather words of sympathy, she pleaded, "Don't tell anyone. The others don't need to know."

"But why? They love you. You don't have to keep it from them."

"It's not that. I don't want to explain."

"Explain?" I was puzzled.

"How relieved I am that she's free of that man! She got back at him by dying. Oh, God, I wish it had been him."

Over time, we'd all shared fragments of our lives with each other. I knew "that man" meant her father, of course. Often regaling us with stories, she told us how her musician parents met on tour when they were accompanying world-famous rock bands. After a surprise pregnancy, they left the life of drugs and casual sex behind them. They found God and traveled the world as missionaries. When Julie talked about them, she'd laugh and say, "Then they tried to beat the devil out of us." Dr. Hastings once asked her, "So what church do you attend?" She grinned and said, "The national parks." Still, she was the apple of her daddy's eye, being the youngest, smartest, and prettiest of his three daughters. He was furious when she married Chet, and that made her happy. I reasoned that she wanted him to see that, unlike her mother, she didn't have to be submissive to a bully.

She freshened her makeup, drew in a deep breath, and turned to me with a weak smile. "Well, she's free at last. I'll celebrate that tonight."

Returning in feigned high spirits, she infused the party with new energy. Standing in the shadows, I recalled the words of Shakespeare:

> Give sorrow words; the grief that does not speak
> Whispers the o'er-fraught heart and bids it break.

Just before midnight, Julie slipped off her gown. Swaying to the music, she made her way to the end of the diving board. Before we could stop her, she performed a perfect swan dive into the unheated pool.

"Come in," she yelled to Dr. Jim. He shook his head and flashed her a disapproving look. Dr. Jim, our superego and lead psychologist on the team, always tried to keep our ids in check, but Julie's free spirt presented a challenge. She teased him gently about his fastidious ways, but we all knew they admired each other.The others gathered around the pool to watch. The pool lights sharpened the outlines of the sensuous somersaults and rolls she made under water. I pulled the cover off the heated Jacuzzi. Like a dolphin, she suddenly surfaced, then leaped into the hot water and let out an exuberant breath of pleasure. Others slipped out of their formal wear and joined her.

A few weeks later, Dr. Hastings stuck his head inside my office. I stopped dictating and invited him in. He shook his head and said, "I'm heading to the Hall. I just wanted to ask a favor." Without waiting, he said, "Keep an eye on Julie." Then he closed the door and left for Juvenile Hall. I'd been self-absorbed—trying to learn the hectic routine of the unit, becoming familiar with the staff, and learning to master my responsibilities—and hadn't spent time with Julie since she returned from her mother's funeral. At times, the demands of the job felt overwhelming. But that was no excuse. I trusted Dr. Hastings's sagacity and felt Julie must be in crisis.

Later in the day, Julie stopped by. Like me, she was still an intern. All psychologists had to undergo three thousand hours of supervision, preferably in a multidiscipline setting such as ours, before sitting for the boards; once we passed the exams, we'd become licensed and then allowed the privilege of solo practice.

"You got a minute?" she asked as she flopped into a chair.

"I've always got time for you," I said, smiling.

"It's about this Rorschach on a mother I evaluated yesterday. It worries me." She handed me the protocol, pointing at the ratio number indicative of suicide potential.

"Wow." I let out a slow, long breath. The number stood out like a flashing red light. Nothing else on the test looked worrisome. It could be an anomaly, a false positive.

"Yeah," she said, agreeing with my sigh. "I'm worried about her. Her little girl was removed from the home due to negligence. I agreed with the social worker's recommendation that the child stay with the foster family until the mother got some counseling."

"What did you sense when you interviewed her? Did she seem depressed? Any history of suicide—by her or a family member?"

"Not according to her. She even agreed with the social worker's case plan. Said that it was probably best. There was something in her voice that troubled me, but I couldn't put my finger on it. It was so flat, so devoid of any emotion."

"Did you run it by Dr. Jim?" I asked.

"He's out at one of the facilities, and I have to turn in the report today."

"Hmm," I murmured. Even bad parents put up a fight and don't surrender their kids that casually. "Look, if she were my client, I'd call her." Depression has many faces and the scariest is indifference. "Explain that you're concerned about her and give her the number of the local mental health clinic. Since a copy of the report goes to her attorney, I'd give him a call too. See if he can urge her into treatment."

Julie nodded.

"And how are you doing?" I asked. "I'm sorry," I stumbled, "but work got in the way. We haven't had a chance to talk since your mother's death. I know you left for a week to go back for the funeral. How did it go?"

"Okay. Fine," she said breezily, "but happiness was Georgia in my rearview mirror." She stood and turned to leave. Just as she got to the door she turned and asked, "Can you get away for some golf this weekend?"

"Can you? You're the one with five kids," I laughed.

"You bet." We set the time and place. Just before leaving, she tossed a zinger: "By the way, I've left Chet. I'll fill you in later." Then she was gone.

We met at a public golf course. Both of us were beginners. Our rowdy, loud whoops and laughter at our lousy shots must have annoyed the nearby players. Soon I felt uneasy; Julie's laughter and exuberance were a little too much for someone who had just lost a mother and left a marriage.

"So, is it really over with Chet?" I asked.

"Yep. It's time I moved on. It's what he wanted, I'm sure, since he was seeing another woman."

"Oh! Where are you staying?" I asked.

"With friends," she answered without elaborating.

"Look, if things don't work out there and you need a place to stay, my home is your home."

"Thanks, but I think I've found my place."

"That sounds interesting," I said, wanting to hear more.

"It's a group of people. They're..." She stopped. "Not now. Later, at the nineteenth hole," she laughed.

By the twelfth tee, Julie was nearing a manic stage. When she stumbled and fell into the sand trap, she rolled over and began making an angel like a kid in the snow. Her frenetic actions communicated desperation.

Later, while sipping wine at the clubhouse, she said casually, "I'm leaving."

"Leaving. What do you mean?"

"I'm quitting the team."

I nearly dropped my wine glass. "You're kidding." I gulped.

"Do you see any hope for the world?" she asked, suddenly becoming serious.

Did she really expect a thoughtful answer after a rowdy golf game and an empty glass of wine? I replied, "Well, considering that over 90 percent of the species that have inhabited this planet have gone extinct, why should man be hopeful? Man's far more reckless, I'd say."

"I agree," she said emphatically. She leaned toward me, her face earnest and intense. "I've met a group of people who are trying to do something about it. They believe nuclear energy is the answer."

Dumbfounded, I said, "Aren't they an extremist group?" I searched my memory, having seen something about them in the papers recently. "Seems I read something about them, about their leader getting into trouble. How did you get hooked up with them?"

"I met them through Chet. I've known them for a while."

That didn't elevate them at all in my mind.

"Does Chet go along with their thinking?" I knew she heard the edge in my voice.

"Not now, especially after I left him and moved into their compound. He thinks they're kooks." Chet's status suddenly increased.

The magnitude of her life decision and the way it came about so suddenly after the death of her mother and the breakup of her marriage troubled me. The psychologist in me finally woke up. *What's going on here? What is this really about?*

"Can we change the subject, Julie?" I asked, "What happened to the case we discussed in my office? The one about the mother with the high suicide indicator on the Rorschach?"

She stirred her drink with a straw and looked deep into the glass. She answered with a tight voice, struggling to hide the tears just behind her eyes. "Do you know what her attorney said when I called him? He said, 'She's a manipulator; I wouldn't worry about her.'"

The drink trembled slightly in her hands. "She did it," she said, almost inaudibly. "She didn't show up for the court hearing." Julie drew in a deep breath and paused. Finally, she turned to me and said, "I'm not cut out for this kind of work. Look, some of us can, and some of us can't. You can, and I admire you for it. But I think I need another line of work."

I argued, "Julie, you're as cut out for it as anyone I know. You are a wonderful evaluator, sensitive and insightful."

"I agree with one word: I am sensitive, very sensitive. I'm going to try something different."

After giving all the standard advice about seeking treatment to deal with losses, I tried another approach. I pleaded, "Look, don't act impulsively. This is an extreme decision. You've recently lost your mother, a client, and your marriage. Don't make the decision to walk away from this career. You just need time. Time to sort everything out." She looked past me, closing the discussion.

She was determined, and nothing any of us on the team said changed her mind. She disappeared, and we heard nothing of her whereabouts. Over time, her sparkling presence faded in my memory, and I grew used to her absence in my life. Still, I sometimes wondered how she was and if she had truly made the right choice. *What a waste,* I thought. She had thrown all that education and training down the drain. I wondered what her real motivation was for leaving. Did she do this to punish her father? Was the suicide of a client enough to send her over the edge?

The next time, and the last time, that I saw Julie, I was returning home from a trip abroad and passing through Los Angeles International Airport. I would have walked by the small group handing out pamphlets had I not recognized the voice. The woman trying to get the attention of passersby was thin and ungroomed; her tangled, unwashed hair and threadbare clothes nearly concealed her beauty. I stopped and stared, making sure it was Julie. Feeling my eyes on her, she turned, and our eyes met.

She looked uneasy as I approached her, but then her bright smile shined on me. "An old friend from the past," she explained to the small gathering. We walked a short distance away.

"Wow, you've changed," I said.

She nodded and replied, "You too."

"Yeah, well, we all get older." We laughed. "So, you're still with the nuclear group?" I asked, glancing down at the stack of pamphlets she held.

"No. I left them years ago. Still looking for my bliss," she laughed. She asked about some of the staff. I told her that Dr. Hastings had died and a new director took over and that I had left to establish a private practice. I handed her my business card.

I asked about her family. She didn't have contact with any of them. She didn't say much about what she was doing when I pressed her. "Oh, you know, just trying to save the world."

Teasingly, I said, "Let me see what cult you're with now," as I reached for one of the pamphlets.

She seemed reluctant to hand it to me; she looked hesitantly toward her group, then her demeanor changed swiftly. I glanced at the material and recognized it was from a radical militia group that had recently attended protests bearing guns. She couldn't help but read the disappointment on my face.

"Well, I've got to get going," she said. "We're not supposed to be handing out stuff here." She laughed. "We're trying to get support for a—"

I cut her off. "Goodbye, Julie." I started to walk away with a heart full of disgust. I heard her say as I turned, "It's not what you think."

I spun around, "No? Then what is it about?" When she began to spout antigovernment rhetoric, I headed for the taxi line. By the time I got there, I was so mad that I decided to go back and talk some sense into her. What did I have to lose? But when I went back to the area where we'd stood, the group had disappeared.

I crossed Julie off my list of friends, considering she was hopeless. I tried to put her out of my mind. A few years later, I read a newspaper account of a shooting that took place among the group mentioned in her pamphlet. The paper listed her as a victim.

Well, she got what she deserved, I told myself, a feeble attempt to assuage my guilt for having left her in their hands.

I thought that was the end of ever hearing about Julie. But I was wrong. A few weeks later, a message was left on my answering machine: "I'd like to speak to you." It was a colleague of Julie's. "She talked a lot about you. She wanted me to give you a message should anything happen to her. Please call." The man left his number.

I had mixed feelings about returning the call. But loyalty is my strongest trait. Finally, I relented, hoping that maybe he could tell me one good bit of information that would soften the anger I felt.

I could hardly breathe after what the caller, a government agent told me.

"Julie couldn't stand the thought of you thinking badly about her. She wanted you to know that after she left the court, she came to work for us. We'd been targeting her since her college days. With her experience in childhood of living in so many foreign countries, she had a perspective we needed. We finally persuaded her to join us after her marriage ended. She became an infiltrator of extremist groups. Her insight and sensitivity were invaluable. She couldn't tell you. She couldn't tell anyone. She sacrificed everything for her country, even giving her life."

I hung up the phone in shock. How easy it is to reach wrong conclusions. *Oh, Julie, forgive me for my misunderstanding.* I thought about the courage and daring it took to do what she did—more than what was required of us in the court.

It gave a whole new meaning to the conversation we had in the bar of the clubhouse years ago, when she said, "Some of us can, and some of us can't."

CHAPTER 3

The Sisters

MARTY BISHOP STOOD IDLY at the window of his office staring into the day room where the girls were cleaning up from breakfast. He watched a staff member count each piece of silverware. Even a spoon could be turned into a weapon. His eyes rested on Ophelia, a svelte, olive-skinned fourteen-year-old Hispanic girl whose almond-shaped eyes made her dark brown irises seem even darker within the clear white sclera. Glancing in his direction, she flashed a coquettish smile, showing off her dimples and straight white teeth. She returned to the task of sweeping up the debris from the morning meal.

A surge of sadness filled him as he studied her. The unfortunate reality of her life, and of others like her who found their way to Juvenile Hall, had inspired in him a will to do good. He himself had once been in similar circumstances, and a chaplain had put him on the right path. Marty followed in his counselor's footsteps. What he wanted more than anything in life was to be good and to do good. He believed that most people wanted that before they were lured away by sinful temptations. That's what he saw happening here. Ophelia was following her sister Maria, and Maria was bad—very bad. He'd tried his best to lead Maria back to the church and restore her to a place of goodness, but he failed. After struggling with the idea, he reluctantly surrendered to the reality that Maria was evil—plain evil.

At that moment, Dr. Jim appeared at the front desk, which was visible from Marty's office. *Just the man I want to see.* The mental health team of psychologists visited the units on a regular basis and made heroic efforts to save kids from suicide and self-destructive behaviors. Marty liked Dr. Jim, even though the girls joked about his homely appearance. His wiry, unkempt hair, large hawklike features, and unathletic build stopped them from using flirtation to hide behind during their counseling sessions. They didn't know he'd been a famous soccer player in Jordan before immigrating to America. Marty envied him, knowing his plainness allowed for more therapy success with the girls. Despite these feelings, he appreciated that Dr. Jim was always generous with advice. And he hoped that Dr. Jim was there to see Maria.

"Dr. Jim, do you have a few minutes for me?"

"Sure, Marty. What's up?"

Before he could answer, they both turned in the direction of an altercation taking place down the hall.

Maria, a sturdy girl with a short-clipped haircut and conspicuous tattoos running down both arms, was giving directions to some of the younger girls.

"Valerie, pick up those books and magazines and put them on the shelf. And Terry, you clean the bathrooms."

Terry whined, "But I did them yesterday. I'm not doing them today."

"Oh, yes you are. You want a little discipline," Maria snarled, sounding like an angry parent talking to a naughty child, flaunting her unmerited authority.

"Cuidado," Ophelia cautioned as a staff member approached.

"No problem. I can handle her." Then Maria added with a voice of command, "You sweep."

The staff member stopped in her tracks and turned to Maria and said sharply, "I told you to sweep, Maria, not Ophelia."

Maria shrugged. "But she does it better than me. Everyone knows that." Defiance shaped every syllable.

"You're right, but it's not what I asked."

Maria put her hand on her hip and boldly snapped back, "Yeah, well, sometimes you ask some pretty stupid things."

"That does it! You are written up and you're busted from going to the Friday night social." The staff member knew how important this event was to the girls. It was part of a trial program newly initiated to give an incentive for good behavior. The social allowed a two-hour period for the girls to mix with the best behaved boys on the unit who were serving light sentences.

"If I don't go, nobody on the unit will go either," she threatened.

Sue Dennison gestured with her hands as if to indicate "It's okay with me." Sue had been a counselor on the unit for about as long as the fixtures had been there. She turned away from Maria, shaking her head, and headed toward Dr. Jim and Marty, who had stood passively watching.

"Lordy, we've lost control of this unit. That girl has been running things too long."

"Why don't you transfer her?" asked Dr. Jim.

"Don't think I haven't tried, but all the other units are filled. I've been ordered to keep her here until the hearing, hopefully next week. We just have to wait it out, I guess."

"Well, from what I just saw, she certainly acted like she was running the show," Dr. Jim added with a sympathetic voice.

"It doesn't matter what we do, and we've tried a variety of punishments. She always gets the upper hand—Maria, along with her little sister, Ophelia. They call themselves the madre and padre of the unit; and all the girls are their niñas, and they must do exactly what they tell them to. The other girls are afraid of her." Sue sighed.

"Most of these girls grew up in the barrio with them. Since Maria was a gang leader there, I imagine they are afraid of what might happen if they don't go along," Dr. Jim reasoned.

"It's more than that," Sue paused. "There's something unnatural about it."

"That's what I want to talk to you about," Marty said to Dr. Jim. "Could we talk in my office?"

The two men were respectful of their separate roles. In fact, Dr. Jim felt indebted to Marty. Sometime back, the Probation Department, led by a few hall staffers, petitioned to keep Mental Health personnel off the units unless there was a specific order by the court. The Probation Department's view was that Mental Health was "too soft": discipline and rehabilitation were in conflict. Marty argued on behalf of the Mental Health Department, seeing its value. The decision to keep the psychologists involved came after a tragic suicide occurred; the court then mandated that Mental Health have full access to the wards. By filling out a form, either a staff member or an inmate could request a visit by the psych team.

The team's responsibilities were even expanded to include weekend coverage.

Dr. Jim's purpose this day was to see three girls. Marty hoped Maria was one of them. Things had been getting a little weird in his counseling sessions with her. For several weeks now he had been experimenting with a new therapy tool, age regression.

Sitting across from Dr. Jim, Marty leaned forward and urgently put forth his concern: "I think Maria is a multiple. And I think she has the devil in her."

"Oh? Well, I have to admit, she's got a little devil in her," Dr. Jim chuckled.

"Oh, no. This is serious. I mean *the devil*. I think she's possessed."

"Come on, Marty. Aren't you getting a little carried away? Look, I know you're a minister and you believe in the power of God and Satan, but—"

"No, it's what she is doing in the therapy. She practically admitted it."

"Okay. Tell me what's happened. What's she been telling you?" Dr. Jim was aware of the fad sweeping the country that anyone with hysterical tendencies or psychosis or compulsive behaviors was being labeled as having "multiple personality disorder." A rare diagnosis that was being liberally applied.

Marty studied his hands. *Maybe I shouldn't tell him. Maybe he doesn't believe in demonic possession.* But Marty trusted Dr. Jim. He was not the kind to judge, not even when Marty described in detail his conversion while in prison, which led him into the ministry. Although Dr. Jim was not a religious man, he seemed to accept that there was a place for God in people's lives. But did he accept the role of Satan?

Despite the doubt, Marty plunged forward. "I've been doing age regression with Maria. In truth, it was Dr. Pam's idea."

Dr. Jim raised his eyebrows. "Dr. Double Vision Pam?" He understood that Marty was referring to Dr. Pam Delany.

Marty shook his head with disappointment. "Not you too. I know everyone thinks she only sees multiples, but she's well trained. They laugh at her, but I think it's professional jealousy. I'm not saying that about you, but I know what people say about her. I'll be honest; I've consulted with her, and, yes, she thinks Maria is a multiple."

"Has she even seen Maria in consultation?"

"No, but I've been taking careful notes and discussing them with her under supervision."

"Well, be careful. In my short professional career, I've seen a few fads come and go. But tell me, what makes you think Maria is possessed?"

Marty drew in a deep breath. "In the beginning things went well. She took to this age regression naturally."

"Naturally," Dr. Jim remarked.

Marty heard the veiled sarcasm. "Of course, I know she's a manipulator. But it wasn't like that." He paused a long time, considering whether he should continue.

"It seemed I was getting results. She remembered so many things in her childhood, recalled in detail the day her mother ordered her father out of the house. She was only four. She described how her mother leaned against the door frame and said to her father as he was leaving, 'Pedro, you may be named after Saint Peter, but you're no rock.'" Marty explained to Dr. Jim, in case he might not know, that Saint Peter was referred to as the rock upon which the Catholic church was founded and that many Hispanic males were named Pedro, after Saint

Peter. He then continued, "After that memory surfaced, Maria became a soft, scared little girl. She even talked about her father and his decline into alcohol and how she then became tough, like the rock her padre could not be. She lost that hard edge when she was having the memory."

"Marty, it sounds like Maria made some good connections. But is it possible that she may have been coming on to you? All the girls are crazy about you; they think you're the best-looking man in the place, and they all talk pretty openly about their fantasies."

Marty's face reddened. If he was being honest, he would have to admit that being in the same room with some of them was at times a test of his faith. They unbuttoned their shirts to expose their breasts to him or sat with spread legs while giving him come-hither looks. But not Maria.

"No, no, no, she's not coming on to me. Just the opposite. She acts and speaks like a man. If you heard her talk and saw how her body takes on manly behavior, you'd be convinced. It's not an act. It's real."

"Now you see why Maria calls herself padre. She's become the father in his absence, the protector of her younger siblings. To recreate a family, she's placed Ophelia in the role of mother, madre. She's letting you see the whole essence of herself. That's not being satanic. It's called acting out," Dr. Jim explained.

"There's more," Marty said. "When I told her that if she came back to God, she could rely on his strength and not have to behave like a man, she looked at me with a coldness I recognized from when I was in the depths of my evilness. Do you know what she said?" He didn't wait, but rushed forward, "'I work against God. He knows who I am.' And her voice was completely different. It was like someone was speaking through her. It frightened me. I felt Satan was in the room. That's not normal, not in a girl brought up Catholic."

"Well, she's been abandoned by people she saw as godlike. Maybe she's in a crisis of faith," Dr. Jim said patiently.

"No matter how I try to make her see the need for God, she just becomes harder. Frankly, she's lost. The girl is evil." Marty's last words spilled out in despair, desperation, and defeat.

"Marty, I like you. I think your heart's in the right place. But it worries me when nonprofessionals start doing therapy. They can get into trouble with transference issues; even professionals can. I think you've gotten all muddled and can't see what's going on here."

His words stung, but out of respect, Marty asked, "So what is going on here?"

"She's just trying to create a loving family that she's never had. It's hard to condemn the sisters for their sense of loyalty and their love for each other. It's easy to see why gang activity has such a hold on desperate young people. And I know she's driving the staff to desperation with her open espousal of lesbianism. They're having a harder time with that than anything else. What about you? How do you feel about her behavior?"

"I think she's lost her soul; that's what I think."

"I don't know about those things. That's your domain. But she's certainly on a destructive track with the staff. She's found the only avenue in which it's safe for her to find love. Isn't that what we're all looking for?"

"You mean lust," Marty said with disgust.

"No, I mean love. Familial love. Look, I'll be willing to see her in therapy, and you continue with issues of faith. Okay?"

The impasse between them settled into Marty's gut, leaving a feeling of indigestion and estrangement. Dr. Jim was right about a lot of things, but he was wrong about Maria. She was a bad girl, an evil girl. Dr. Jim could see her in treatment, but Marty didn't think he'd change Maria. It was then that Marty made up his mind about the moral need to separate Maria from vulnerable Ophelia, and it had to be done quickly.

Later, Marty wondered if he'd done the right thing. Ophelia was forlorn and inconsolable. She hadn't shown one dimpled smile since Maria was sent to the California Youth Authority (CYA). Finding it too difficult to endure her hard stares and mean looks filled with such great sadness and hatred, he decided to leave his job as chaplain and join Dr. Delany in her private practice.

Marty had gone behind Dr. Jim's back and urged Maria's probation officer to have her evaluated by Dr. Delany. The adversarial hearing had Dr. Delany on one side and Dr. Jim on the other. Dr. Jim argued against the diagnosis of multiple personality disorder and explained Maria's behavior on the unit in the same terms he used with Marty. He didn't think Maria was suitable for CYA. Her crimes were petty, but he conceded that she was sophisticated for her age and exerted a strong influence on her peers, both in the Hall and in her neighborhood. He also agreed that she would return to gang activities if returned to the community.

Dr. Delany found Maria to be too disturbed to be in any treatment program offered by the juvenile court. She argued that it would be in Maria's best interest, for her own protection and for the protection of the community, for her be sent to CYA, where she could receive treatment in their psychiatric unit for her multiple personality disorder. With professional passion, she defended her diagnosis and stated the need to separate Maria from Ophelia.

Marty attended the hearing. He didn't hold it against Dr. Jim for having an opposing view. This was the way of the court. But he was proud of his affiliation with Dr. Pam, as he affectionately called her. He would have argued the same as she did, but he didn't have a license that qualified him as an expert. Also, he upheld the sacrosanct client-therapist privilege. He consoled himself that although Ophelia might not forgive him right away, she would in the future. She had a chance to become good by his having done good on her behalf.

A few weeks later, Marty ran into Dr. Jim outside the court building. Marty was there to meet a staff member and have lunch with her. He greeted Dr. Jim warmly. After a few formalities, Dr. Jim said, "It's too bad about Ophelia."

"About what?"

"She took her life. She'd been cheeking pills we'd given her for depression. Even though she was on suicide watch at bedtime, she managed to swallow a two weeks' supply without it being observed. The staff assigned to check in on her through the night thought she was sleeping quietly. She died during the night."

Marty paled. Standing speechless, he searched for something within that would stabilize his balance. Finally, he seized upon a rationalization: "At least Ophelia is saved from Maria's fate."

CHAPTER 4

Fire and Chess

DR. ALBERT HASTINGS PRESSED the buzzer beside the steel door that would grant him entrance to the admitting unit of Juvenile Hall. A small screened window permitted him to view down the long hallway. A desk with a button that controlled the lock allowed staff to admit a visitor without having to walk the long distance to the door. Earl, a senior staff member, leaned over the desk, casually flipping the pages of a magazine, ignoring the buzzer. Dr. Hastings was tempted to buzz again, but he knew it would only increase Earl's passive aggressiveness.

He waited patiently for entrance to Unit A, where new wards were screened before being sent to an appropriate unit. Older boys, repeat offenders, or first-timers arrested for a serious crime were sent to Unit B. Most of these boys were headed to the California Youth Authority, the last stop before prison. Younger boys, ages ten through twelve, went to Unit C. Unit D was reserved for lightweight offenders waiting to serve their sentences at a camp or a facility. Then there was Unit X, the mental health unit for kids who had fried their brains on drugs or were psychotic or were serious suicide risks. Each time Dr. Hastings entered Unit X, he softly paraphrased Dante: "I had not thought so many were undone."

Finally, Earl's authoritarian voice, laced with irritation and disrespect, came over the speaker: "Yeah? State your name and business." Even though he knew who was at the door, exercising his authority gave him pleasure.

"Dr. Hastings to see Ronnie Young."

Before Earl could buzz him in, a female staff member approached. She flashed him a bright smile as she opened the door and cheerfully greeted him. Most of the staff were unlike Earl and welcomed Mental Health's presence in the Hall—especially on Unit A. Many first-time offenders, especially the young ones, were often so frightened that they resorted to self-injury.

Ronnie's chart revealed that the twelve-year-old had been booked yesterday afternoon and was awaiting a hearing before being sent to Unit C. His offense was that he had started a fire in a canyon that destroyed five homes. According to the police report, he was seen running from the area; when questioned, he confessed. The day notes by the staff reported that he barely ate supper and was withdrawn and tearful. At bedtime, after the steel door of his five-by-six-foot cell slammed closed, panic set in and he banged and screamed to be let out. A note by the night staff indicated that Ronnie spent the night standing beside his locked door, his face pressed against the small window. He kept repeating, "I have to go home." An evaluation by Mental Health was requested.

"You seeing Crybaby?" Earl asked.

Dr. Hastings nodded. "Is the consultation room in use? I'd like to see him there."

"It's in use. You can see him over there." Earl pointed to the couch in the day room. It wasn't private, but most of the kids were in school, and besides, he wasn't there to talk about Ronnie's crime. It was the court's job to determine guilt or innocence. His job was to help Ronnie cope with this frightening experience and to develop insight into his behavior.

Dr. Hastings's friend George Baker, who once ran Juvenile Hall, shared his philosophy: "We're all a team trying to make a stay in Juvenile Hall an experience that if not pleasant, could at least provide an opportunity for self-examination and growth." Earl embraced the part about making it not pleasant. He unlocked the door to Ronnie's room. The general rule was not to interview kids in their rooms—ostensibly for the visitor's protection should an inmate attack, attempt escape, or bring false allegations against the visitor. Often Dr. Hastings ignored the directive, but because of Ronnie's age, he figured that just getting the boy out of his room would do wonders for his mental health.

Dr. Hastings noted a small red-headed boy, who looked closer to age nine than twelve. His feet swung nervously, and his face was swollen from crying. His hands were busy angrily twisting a piece of paper that Dr. Hastings recognized as a summary of the charges filed against him.

"Hi, Ronnie, I'm Dr. Hastings. Can we talk in the day room? It's brighter there."

Ronnie began to sob, "I have to go home. Will you tell them to let me go home?"

Dr. Hastings patiently waited for Ronnie to rise. "We'll talk about that in the day room."

Ronnie eagerly followed the doctor to the couch. Once seated, he repeated, "Are you going to tell them I need to go home?"

"No. That will be up to the court to decide. I'm here to listen and try to help you not feel so upset."

"But I have to go home," he said in a desperate voice.

"You'll be going to a hearing this afternoon or tomorrow. Has anyone told you when your hearing is?"

"They don't tell me anything."

"Has anyone been to see you? An attorney? Your family?"

Ronnie shrugged. He'd not likely be able to distinguish between an attorney and another staff member.

"Did someone give you their card when they came to talk to you?"

Ronnie fished in his pants pocket and produced a crumpled card. The public defender had visited.

"What about your mom and dad? Have they come?"

His sobbing increased to asthmatic gasping. He shook his head and said, "Nobody." He could barely get out the word.

Dr. Hastings pulled a handkerchief from his pocket and handed it to Ronnie. Ronnie blew his nose several times, and after each blow, he looked pleadingly at Dr. Hastings and repeated, "I have to go home." When he got no reassurance, he flung himself down on the couch and covered his face in his small, skinny arms. Dr. Hastings wanted to hold him and give him comfort. But the boy was beyond comfort, and Dr. Hastings could make no promise that would console him.

"I know you miss home. Tell me about home." A good reflective response could be useful when one has nothing else to offer.

"My sister needs me," Ronnie said with a muffled sob.

"Can't your mom look after her until your situation gets cleared up?"

"She can't. She works a shift from three to eleven." Trying to make the doctor understand, he pleaded, "I have to make her supper and get her to bed."

"Maybe your mom can arrange for someone to do that for your sister."

"You don't understand." Ronnie's voice rose in panic, causing Earl to rush to the door. Dr. Hastings waved him away indicating everything was under control. "She won't let them. She won't let no one help her but me."

"Why is that, Ronnie?"

"Because of the way she is. People can't understand her. Even Mom. Only me. I'm the only one who knows what she wants."

"Can she feed herself?"

Ronnie shook his head.

"How old is she?" Dr. Hastings asked.

"Seven, no eight. She just turned eight."

Clearly, she had a major impairment of some sort. Dr. Hastings wondered how many years Ronnie had been looking after his sister.

"What's wrong with her, Ronnie? Was she always like this? Or did something happen? An accident?"

"She's was born that way." Then he tried his urgent plea again, "Send me home. I have to find out if she's all right. I have to take care of her."

"How about my calling your mom and asking her how your sister is and if someone is helping her. I'll come back and tell you what she tells me."

"No!" he blurted. Then in tears he mumbled, "She'll be mad when she finds out."

His behavior changed. He became quiet and stared at the floor. He looked terribly frightened.

"Why will your mom be mad?"

Ronnie didn't answer, but the rapid swinging of his legs led Dr. Hastings to suspect something. He took a stab: "Did you do something your mom told you not to? And you'll be in big trouble with her? Is it about your sister?"

Ronnie's eyes widened as though God had just caught him in a wrongful act. A look of "How did you know?" spread across his face and his eyes searched Dr. Hastings's face. He seemed to be wondering if he could trust him with his secret. Then he cracked as though he'd been under interrogation and began to confess how he ended up in Juvenile Hall.

"She didn't get to see the fireworks. She was sick. Miguel brought some to school and I bought them from him— pinwheels, sparklers, and a Mount Vesuvius. I didn't want to light them in the backyard because the neighbors would tell. So, I pushed her to the top of the levee, by the woods where we sometimes go." He paused. Doubt clouded his face.

"What do you mean you pushed her?"

"In her wheelchair." He started to cry again. "I'm not supposed to take her outside. But she likes the woods. She likes to hear the water in the creek."

Dr. Hastings could see the scenario unfold in his mind. He felt for the boy. He thought of his own grown children and wondered how they had escaped unscathed from the escapades of childhood.

"You've taken her there before?"

"Only two times. Mom found out the second time and I got the strap. But I knew Carrie would like to see the colors. I told her about the fireworks. She wanted to see them."

"How far away from the house did you take her?"

"To the levee, not far. I didn't take her into the gully. I left her on top and climbed down."

It wasn't Dr. Hastings's job to interrogate or even to know the details of the crime. But he couldn't stop himself from asking, "What happened when you got there?"

"Mount Vesuvius blew up. It headed for a tree across the creek."

Dr. Hastings asked, "So you want to go home to make sure she doesn't tell your mom that you took her there? So you won't get in trouble with your mom?"

Very bad psychiatry, Dr. Hasting said to himself. *Never voice a conclusion before the client comes to it.* Even though Ronnie's confession would not be included in Dr. Hastings's summary of the session, he envisioned the district attorney calling him as a witness. That's why he never wanted the kids to tell him about their involvement in a crime. Was his job to have the boy accept the reality of his situation? Should he say, "You caused a big fire; now a lot of people are really mad at you and want to make sure you don't go home for a long, long time"?

Before he could answer his own question, Ronnie was speaking. "I was pushing Carrie hard, trying to get home. She fell out of the chair. Someone stopped to help me. We could see the smoke in the sky. The man helped me get Carrie home. He must have told the police where I lived. They came and took me here."

"Did the police know Carrie was in the house?"

He shrugged. "I hid her. When I saw their car, I put her in the big closet and told her not to be afraid, that I'd come back for her. I promised her. I have to go home and make sure she's okay."

Dr. Hastings patted Ronnie's arm, offering comfort. "I'm sure your mom's discovered Carrie by now and made arrangements for her care. I'll call your mom and find out how Carrie is. Then I'll come back and talk with you again this afternoon."

Dr. Hastings had made up his mind to recommend that Ronnie be transferred ASAP to Unit C. There he would have more freedom on the unit, spend less time in his room, and adjust faster. It wasn't likely he'd be going home anytime soon.

"Ronnie, I'm going to ask that you be transferred to another unit. There are kids your age and you'll have more activities. I just need to make a phone call. Get your stuff together and I'll walk you over as soon as I can arrange it."

Since Ronnie's hearing had been postponed until the following day because of a filled court calendar, his assigned probation officer agreed to the transfer after talking by phone to Dr. Hastings. While the doctor and the boy stood in the hall waiting for Earl to arrange the transfer, another charge was being admitted. A handsome Hispanic boy, handing over his personal items, placed his wallet on the desk. Earl picked it up and whistled at a picture inside. "My girl," the boy said.

Earl studied the picture. "Yeah, I know her. She's sweet. I had her last night."

The boy drew back his fist and slammed it into Earl's face. Staff started running in their direction, a whistle sounded, and the words "lock down" were yelled through the hall. Nearby inmates lingered to watch before being ordered to their rooms.

Earl and three other large male staffers wrestled the new boy to the floor.

Dr. Hastings shook his head. It was so typical of Earl to find pleasure in setting off a youngster just so he could bully him. He had as much maturity and wisdom as the kid who had fallen for the insult.

Ronnie edged closer to Dr. Hastings, his eyes wide with fear. "Listen, Ronnie, the game is not to let someone push your buttons. You have to be smart about these things."

Later, in a telephone call, Ronnie's mother told Dr. Hastings how scared she was for Ronnie. "He loves his sister and she's heartbroken that he's not here. He's a good boy, but he just doesn't think. If only he'd learn to stop and think before he acts."

After the call, Dr. Hastings visited Ronnie in his new unit. He assured him that Carrie was fine and his mother would be visiting—and that she wasn't so mad as to stop loving him.

Mattie, the large, maternal senior staff member on the unit, said to Dr. Jim, "That boy is going to have trouble. He just doesn't think before he acts."

Dr. Hastings observed Ronnie watching a checkers game between two other wards. He walked over to the cabinet where the games were stored. He pulled out a chess set and set it up at the other end of the room and motioned for Ronnie to join him.

He explained the rules of the game and they began to play. They played every day for six weeks until Ronnie learned to think before making a move.

CHAPTER 5

Achy Breaky Heart

HAVE YOU THOUGHT RECENTLY about the magic of memory? Isn't it remarkable how the smallest stimulus can trigger a powerful, unexpected response? A mild breeze recreates the happiness of a summer afternoon in childhood; a crisp starry night, the remembrance of a first kiss; the scent of a passerby's perfume, a chapter in a romance. And the tune of a song can transport us to the past.

Such a transposition occurred to me when I heard Billy Ray Cyrus singing "Achy Breaky Heart." The song stirred a long-forgotten memory, and I was suddenly back in my office at the juvenile court.

Four-year-old Ryan sat on the sofa in my office. His large dark eyes, empty of expression, were fixed on me. He rocked slowly back and forth, humming softly to himself. He'd been through this before.

"You like to sing?" I asked.

He nodded.

"I like music too. Would you sing for me?"

As if he were auditioning, he rose, stood tall, threw back his shoulders, and with a clear, strong voice sang, "Achy Breaky Heart." However, Ryan altered the last words of the chorus to "He might just grow up and kill a man." Sadly, because of Ryan's heartbreaking background, I hoped that it was only a case of misunderstood lyrics and not a foreshadowing of his future.

Handsome little Ryan was referred to me by Social Services for psychotherapy. Two separate times a family member had pinned a note on his shirt and abandoned him, once at a police station, once at a park. *He might just grow up and kill a man.*

I met many children while working as a psychologist for the juvenile court. Locked in my heart are tales of even darker crimes against children. But those stories are theirs to tell when they are ready.

One situation nearly broke my heart, and I often wonder about it. It was a case of torn love. The memory arose one day when I caught the scent of a passing woman's cologne.

In my office at the juvenile court building, I welcomed what we called a quiet day, a day offered to staff to catch up on dictation and charting. This day there would be no evaluations, no treatment cases. Luxuriating in the thought of an undisturbed day, I dreaded giving the morning over to the Dictaphone. The phone rang, jolting me out of a daze. Karen, an attorney for County Council, was on the line.

"We have a delicate situation here. It needs a delicate touch. We have a little boy called Conner in my office; however, his real name is Kyle. We've just discovered he was kidnapped several years ago. His mother is in the building. We thought it would be best if a psychologist helped with the reunification. We'd prefer a female psychologist and the judge wants you to do it."

It was so like Karen to resort to flattery when she wanted to squeeze a favor out of someone. She was as tragic as some of the cases we saw. I'd been shocked by the transformation in her over the years—from a lithe, youthful advocate to a chain-smoking, jaded, hardened attorney. Sometimes I worried that one day I'd look in the mirror and see the same streaks of agony lining my face.

She gave a brief summary of the situation. The child's father was headed for prison for having kidnapped the boy. He disappeared from the marriage four years ago, taking two-year-old Kyle with him. Sometime later he met a French girl, who was in the country illegally and was soon to be deported. The problem, the attorney explained, was that Conner/Kyle believed this French woman to be his mother. From two and half years of age he had lived with her. He was now six. During a routine traffic stop, the officer discovered that Kyle was a "missing child." His actual mother had just arrived in the court building from Massachusetts.

"I'll be right down," I said breezily. *This should only take an hour of my time*, I reasoned, and I'd do anything to postpone dictating. "I'll meet Kyle first, and assess his emotional state. Then I'll meet with the mother and reunite them."

Karen paused. When she spoke again, her voice sounded cautious: "Sure. Kyle is with Esme, the one he thinks is his mother. They are waiting for you in the conference room."

I opened the door to where Kyle and Esme were waiting. Unprepared, I stepped inside a Raphael-like painting of Madonna and Child. The dark-haired boy leaned against the body of a youthful, slim, angelic-looking mother figure. The love that radiated between them came at me like a tidal wave. I stepped back into the hall and closed the door. I took a deep breath. There was something sacred in that room, and I felt as though I was Lucifer sent to disturb it.

I decided instead to meet the child's mother first. Margaret, an impatient, brusque woman, rose quickly as I entered. Pain had etched hard lines on her face.

"Are you the doctor who's to bring my son to me?" Her tone was demanding. "What's the holdup? I've waited four years for this moment. I plan to take him home this afternoon. I have plane reservations, so we need to wrap this up quickly, Doctor."

"I understand how you must feel, but this may not be easy for your son. Are you prepared for his not remembering you? For the attachment he may feel toward the woman he believes is his mother?"

"That bitch! How can she live with herself? I'll explain everything to him. In time, he'll get over her."

I told her that I needed to prepare Kyle first for the meeting with her. "Please be patient until I return." I braced myself as I reentered the room where Kyle waited with Esme.

Seemingly sensing danger when I entered, Kyle moved closer to Esme.

"Have you told him why he's here?" I asked Esme.

She shook her head; tears filled her eyes. "I can't. I can't leave him," she said in a whisper.

Kyle climbed on her lap, "Mommy, don't cry. What does the lady want you to tell me?" His voice was brave, but his face was pale with anxiety.

"I think you're the only one who can explain it to him," I said to her.

She nodded. She stood him in front of her, and then knelt and placed her hands on his face. "I love you. Never forget that," she said tenderly. In an even, quiet voice, she told him that he had another mother, one before her, who also loved him. The doctor was going to take him to meet her, and he would be going to live with his other mother.

He began to cry; between the sobs he pleaded, "Don't leave me, Mommy. Don't go away. You come with me."

Esme explained how that was not possible. She told him about the day that she met him and his father in the motel where she worked—how she believed that he had no mother and how happy she was to become his mother. Kyle continued to sob, softly repeating over and over, "No. No. You can't go away. You can't go away." She struggled to ease his inconsolable grief.

During the next hour, Esme, Kyle, and I talked about many things. Kyle said he didn't remember having another mother. When he seemed able to grasp the reality of his plight, I asked if he'd like to meet her. He nodded but threw his arms around Esme's neck. I left them alone and went to talk with Margaret.

"The news has been shocking and traumatic for Kyle and he's devastated about being separated from Esme," I told her. I explained the importance of having Esme present to help with the reunification as she had no part in the kidnapping.

She resisted, stating angrily, "She has no rights here! No rights at all, Doctor."

I replied firmly but in a calm voice: "To tell you the truth, at this moment I'm not really concerned about either of your rights. I'm only thinking of Kyle's. I want to make it as easy for him as I can."

We seemed to have a standoff: we stared at each other with determination to have it our way. Finally, Margaret nodded. "Okay, but let's make it quick. I don't know if I can bear being in her presence."

"I understand how hard this is for you. Please, for the moment, can we only think about how hard this might be for Kyle?"

As we entered the room, Margaret rushed toward Kyle, reaching for him to take him in her arms, to take him from Esme, but he burrowed his face in Esme's bosom and began to cry.

She pleaded with him: "I've bought you a pony. Would you like a pony? Wait till you see your room. It's full of toys, games, and—many other things—cars, cap guns."

"He doesn't like guns," Esme said softly.

In Margaret's desperation to win him over, she rushed on. Kyle kept his eyes closed and his face against Esme's chest.

Several times Esme urged him to go to his mother, to look at her, but he refused. Slowly the two women began to acknowledge each other, and they began to talk.

Esme informed her, "He likes a light on at night."

"Did he ever ask about me?"

"He was so little. I don't think he remembered."

The morning became afternoon as the two mothers sat and talked together. I ignored the conference room's ringing phone, knowing it was the attorney wondering what was happening. When I walked out of the room hours later, the two women had worked out an agreement to spend a few days to let Kyle become acquainted with his mother and say goodbye to Esme.

The judge said it was the most unusual court order he'd ever written, granting that it was an unusual situation.

Several weeks later I ran into Karen on another matter. "How did you do it?" she asked me. "How did you get them to agree?"

"I didn't do anything. It was Kyle."

When Kyle finally approached his mother and stood timidly beside her, he said, "You smell like flowers." And that was the beginning of his memory awakening. He didn't remember his mother's face or her touch or her voice. But he remembered her smell. That's when he was able to climb on her lap. That's when she softened and agreed to give Kyle the time he needed to say goodbye to Esme.

"Have you heard how it's working out for him?" I asked Karen.

"We got a letter from the mother thanking us for helping her through a rough time. I think that kid might just make it. She even lets Kyle write 'Aunt Esme.' Can you believe it? People are nuts."

I smiled because I knew that Karen loved this kind of nuttiness.

My memory of that day was awakened when a woman walking by smelled like flowers, the same fragrance that Kyle's mother wore. One never knows what will trigger a memory, but I think it's a wonderful part of the way we are designed.

CHAPTER 6

A Christmas Miracle

MRS. JENSEN LEANED FORWARD, urgently conveying her purpose: "Doctor, you are our last hope. Unless you can help us, we'll have to return her."

The referral had come from a social worker who thought I could work miracles—she referred adoption cases on the brink of unraveling. Sadly, many couples waited years for a child and when they finally got one, it was not what they expected—a little like real life.

The mother continued. "The problem is Shirley is too perfect." Her hand fell in exasperation. "I know you must think we're crazy. Every parent wants a perfect child. But she's too good. It's like having a doll—or a guest—in one's house, not a real, imperfect, messy child." She looked at me anxiously.

"How long have you had her? And what history were you given about her?"

"A year and a half. We only know that she came into the system at the age of two. Her mother voluntarily gave her up, preferring her drugs, most likely. Shirley spent about two years in foster care. Circumstances caused her to be moved a few times, but we don't know the reasons why. She was placed with us at the age of four."

The attractive, well-groomed mother hesitated and then added, "You see, my husband and I have talked a lot about this. She's just not normal. We've agreed to give therapy a try, but if she's not making progress by the end of the year"—she gave a long, tortured sigh—"we'll have to turn her back to Social Services." Tears gathered in her eyes. A painfully long pause followed before she said, "It's not that we can't love her, it's that we don't think she's capable of loving us."

Glancing at the calendar I saw that I had a little over eight weeks to see if I could help Shirley make a genuine connection.

"You're not giving me much time to work a miracle," I told her.

When I met Shirley, a petite, lovely robot stood before me. Her dazzling, eager smile and large, sparkling eyes shined like small planets. She offered her hand and in a grown-up voice said, "It's very nice to meet you." She selected a chair and after sitting crossed her legs, folded her hands, and with the same polite voice asked, "Are we going to have a conversation?"

The unnaturalness of her manner threw me. It seemed she had been through this before, and I didn't think I'd find out what I needed by talking. Gathering my thoughts, I replied, "No. I'd rather we play."

A small frown appeared on her face like a cloud crossing the sun, and then it quickly disappeared. She decided on a coloring book and a box of crayons from the shelf. I chose two dollhouses, one for her and one for me. Placing them side by side on the floor, I selected moms and dads, several children, furniture, and household items for each house.

Throughout the session, Shirley continued coloring, ignoring me while I made up stories and played with my dolls. My child dolls were unpredictable, at times demanding and other times affectionate. Acting out the role of the parent dolls, I was sometimes reasonable, sometimes impatient, and sometimes loving. I invited her several times to join me, but she politely declined: "I'd rather color."

During our second session, she occasionally turned in my direction while she was coloring—watching but not reacting. I tried engaging her with a question: "Do you remember living in another house?" Her large eyes stared hard at me and then she turned back to her coloring book; however, I noticed that it took a while for her to begin coloring again.

At the end of our third meeting, Shirley left her coloring book; she stood pensively above me, watching as I fed and bathed the children and placed them in bed. She observed with a gravity, as if she was studying how to get it right. She picked up the baby's bottle, stuck it in her own mouth, pretended to suck on it, and then handed it back to me. Happily I thought, *Something is beginning to happen.*

I walked to the waiting room with her, wearing a smile. Shirley greeted her mother in her usual polite and mechanical manner.

Later that day, Mrs. Jensen phoned: "Doctor, we don't see any improvement. In fact, she seems worse. I mean, she's even more unfeeling. We're not sure we want to go through the Christmas holidays like this."

Hearing her despair, I reminded her that we agreed to wait until the end of the year.

"Do you see any improvement, Doctor?" she asked.

"It's early. Please be patient. Give her some more time," I pleaded.

The next week, Shirley ran into the office and immediately located the two dollhouses. "This is yours and this is mine," she announced.

I expected her children and mother to be perfect. But to my surprise, Shirley became severe and destructive with her children. She ordered them to bed without food; she threw them out of the house and made them sleep outside on the cold ground without blankets. When one of my child dolls went over to her house to visit, she announced in a stern voice, "No visitors allowed!"

I asked, "When can I come to play at your house?"

"Never. My children are bad, and they will learn to be good."

Now we're getting somewhere, I thought thankfully.

Little seemingly perfect Shirley turned out to be a cruel, harsh, and negligent mother! But I only observed her and continued to play the part of a nurturing parent with the dolls in my care.

The following week, things got worse. Shirley's house became topsy-turvy, with furniture piled on top of the children. Confusion and chaos dominated her small domain. When one doll misbehaved, she tore off its arm and she pulled off the head of another doll after a minor infraction. Was she testing me? Waiting for a reaction from me? This was a mother in need of help.

I picked up a toy telephone and said, "It sounds like there's a problem over there. Can I come over and help?" But she said, "No, thank you. No visitors allowed." Then toward the end of the session, she violently tossed a child doll aside, and it landed near me. Gathering it up and cuddling it, I said, "You're so little. So little and scared. You can sleep in my bed, and I won't let anyone hurt you."

Following this session, I called Mrs. Jensen and asked her if we could increase the sessions to two times a week as the year's end was nearing and I needed more time with Shirley. She reluctantly agreed and offered that she didn't see any change in Shirley's behavior at home.

For the next few sessions, we sat side by side: Shirley, playing in her world, and I, playing in mine. Occasionally she glanced in my direction. At the end of our seventh week, she offered me one of her dolls, asked if I would wrap it in a blanket and feed it, and then insisted that I sing to her baby. I did. Shirley lay down on the floor and covered herself with a blanket as I sang Christmas carols to the doll.

Realizing I had only one more week before Christmas, I worried that the Jensens might cancel sessions because of the holidays. Something significant was happening in our play, and it would be tragic if the therapy was ended or interrupted. I needn't have worried.

While waiting for Shirley to arrive for her next appointment, I finished reading an article on the significance of smell. The doctor doing the research talked about the differences between men and women in their response to odors. Males were aroused by the smell of pumpkin and cinnamon, but females responded most strongly to the smells of cucumbers and licorice.

Shirley ran into the office without waiting for me to greet her in the waiting room. She grabbed the blanket off the couch and standing before me asked in a shy voice, "Can I be your baby today?"

I spent the session swaddling her in a blanket and singing the few lullabies and baby songs I could recall. She sucked her thumb, played peekaboo, and most importantly, snuggled into my arms. Regressing, she risked accepting love.

At the end of the hour, she walked into the waiting room, where her mother was sitting. She entered as though still in a dream. She climbed onto her mother's lap, nestled her face against her mother's neck, and said, "Mommy, you smell like cucumbers."

Neither of them could appreciate the significance of Shirley's words.

The day before Christmas, Mrs. Jensen called. She left a message, "Doctor, we had a crisis. Could you call me?"

My heart sank with dread. I'd failed! They were returning her. Preparing myself to do everything I could to persuade them to change their minds, I returned the call.

Mrs. Jensen answered the phone. "I'm so glad you called. You've given us the best Christmas present ever. Last night, Shirley threw a horrible temper tantrum because she wanted to stay up late. We needed to finish wrapping presents, and when we told her no, she went wild. I've never seen such a fit. It scared us at first. After it was over, she broke down and cried and asked me to get down her suitcase from the closet. I asked why she wanted it. She said, 'To pack. I know you'll send me away because I was bad.'"

Softly sobbing, Mrs. Jensen said, "I told her, 'We will never send you back. You're ours forever, even through the bad times.' And do you know what she did? She hugged me, and it felt real. Honestly, Doctor, this is like a Christmas miracle."

CHAPTER 7

Shadows

WHENEVER I HEAR THE phrase "She wasn't always like this," I think of Helen. I was young when I first heard it and was just beginning to understand its awkward meaning.

My job at the time was evaluating clients for conservatorship. When an individual can no longer manage his or her daily affairs and someone petitions the state to provide for the person's care, a legal process takes place, including an evaluation and a court hearing. Because the woman I was sent to evaluate was an escape risk, she was being detained in a locked facility pending the outcome of a court hearing. While waiting in the lobby for the residents to finish lunch, I noted how worn and neglected the facility appeared. Institutional yellow walls, frayed floral carpet, and an antiseptic smell made me glad to be an outsider. Glancing into the dining room, I spotted in a far corner, tucked inside an alcove, a rundown upright piano looking lonely.

"You think they'd mind if I played while they ate?" I asked the receptionist.

"Do whatever you like." She shrugged, displaying a shabby attitude reflecting the place.

Trying to acquaint myself with the forsaken instrument, I discovered the upper-octave B-flat key was stuck and the soft pedal wasn't working. Other than that, the piano had a nice sound and lively action. The dining room fell silent as the timid strains of "Clair de Lune" drifted into the room. At the section where moonlight ripples on water (my interpretation), I heard a chair scrape across the floor. Then a cane urgently tapped its way toward me. I looked up, expecting to hear words of gratitude for bringing the hue of music to a colorless room. Instead, a spry gray-haired woman dressed in an elegant but frayed garment adorned with a faded, fringed scarf stood scowling. She shook her cane as she addressed me sternly: "Young lady, you need to take lessons."

With that, she turned and walked away, shaking her head and mumbling, "Pianissimo!" I knew it meant that she wanted to hear the piece played softly, very softly, as soft as moonlight. She was out of earshot before I could explain about the defective pedal. As I left the piano, the small gathering in the dining room booed the woman and begged me to continue, but I was too deflated to continue.

That was my introduction to Helen, the very person I'd come to evaluate for the court. According to the history given by neighbors and collected from previously filed complaints, Helen was having considerable difficulties: forgetting to pay bills, forgetting to buy groceries, getting lost, spending money on long bus rides, and arriving at destinations without funds for a return fare. Helen's penchant for wandering finally caused her to lose her freedom. The last incident, the one that brought me to see her, happened after a concerned officer at the bus station noticed her looking bewildered and lost. She became combative and increasingly confused upon questioning. That episode eventually brought her to the attention of the public guardian's office, and Helen became a candidate for conservatorship. Before seeing her, I reviewed the day chart at the nursing station and learned that Helen had made numerous attempts to escape.

In her room, I found her sitting at a small table staring vacantly out the window. I explained that I was the psychologist sent to evaluate her for the upcoming court hearing regarding her confinement.

"Well, I don't belong here. You tell the judge that, young lady," she commanded, as if by having ordered it, it would be done.

"It seems you've been having some problems lately. Can you tell me about how you came to be here?" I asked gently.

"I've no problems. The problem is this place. They don't serve fruit. How can a person stay healthy in a place like this? You've got to get me out of here. I don't belong here. This place will kill me."

"Can you tell me about your recent travels? I see you've been quite a few places: Boise, Seattle, Boston, Cleveland." Having read her chart, I knew that these were cities, among others, where she had encounters with officials and ended up in custody. The record noted that she had managed to escape from officials several times.

She turned her back to me as she walked to the window, a proud, dignified walk assisted by a cane. "I was going home," she replied, as though speaking to herself. Staring out on a vacant lot, she dismissed me with her silence.

I pressed on, trying to engage her: "Have you lived in those places?"

Without turning, she replied softly, "The world is my home." Then the agitated voice returned: "I've got to get out of here. I've got to get to New York." She stabbed the floor with her cane, emphasizing the urgency.

"What's in New York? Family?" I asked.

"Wouldn't you rather be in New York than here?" she replied.

I smiled. "I don't know. I've never been there. What's there that I should see?"

"The Met." Then she added, "I don't want to talk to you. You're not going to help me get out."

"I'll try," I offered. "Is there family? Can I call someone for you—someone you can stay with, someone to help you?"

She didn't answer.

Scanning her chart, I saw there was a son named Claude but no address. "Your son, do you have a number for him? Would you mind if I called him?"

"He's got his life. But you can tell him I need fruit." Then to my surprise, she reached in the pocket of her skirt and handed me a wrinkled, soiled piece of paper. I saw an international code preceding the telephone number. During the rest of the interview, she stayed fixed on two things: fruit and getting out.

That night I called Switzerland. How faint and thin the line seemed. I only hoped the familial tie was strong. The public guardian's office directs us to never induce guilt to coax a family member to assume care. We should never presume to know the tenor of a family's heart.

Introducing myself, I told Claude that I was calling to let him know his mother was in protective custody and explained my role as evaluator. I heard a long breath, which sounded like a sigh of relief, over the line.

"She's having difficulty managing her daily affairs," I said.

"Yes, this is not the first time she's been picked up," he offered. After a long pause, he added, as though he wanted me to understand, "She wasn't always like this."

I waited for him to tell me what she had been like. But he changed the subject. As Helen had warned me, he had a life and no, he couldn't take over her care. He gave enough information for me to tell the court that there was no alternate provider. But his impassive voice held me on the line.

"She scolded me today," I laughed, embarrassed at my reluctance to hang up. "She told me I needed to take piano lessons. I was tinkering on the piano in the dining room."

"Yes—well, she was a concert pianist in her day; she played in cities around the world," he said in a matter-of-fact voice. He didn't volunteer more. We hung up.

She was not always like this: a concert pianist! Had her travels, the demands of her profession, brought about this estrangement? Was it even estrangement? My training had instilled the caution to not assume, not guess, and not construe. But I could not forget the wanderer or her desperation for freedom. What was she seeking in her wanderings?

When in the area, and sometimes driving out of my way, I would bring Helen a mango or an orange or strawberries. In exchange she would give me a piano lesson. Listening to me trying to play pianissimo on a honky-tonk keyboard tested her patience. In time, however, a measure of regard grew between us.

One day while guiding me through *Moonlight Sonata*, she said wistfully, "My life, it's been like water in a cupped hand: a brief quench of thirst, so quick to evaporate."

"You must have had some wonderful times. You played in the greatest halls of music."

"Music was my life," she reflected. "Maybe I made mistakes placing it above everything else. But it was the only thing that made me feel complete." With a bewildered look, she added, "I don't know how I became so lost. How did I get here?"

I never fully understood that either, for she would not tell me. Nor did I uncover the dynamics between her and her son. She never spoke of him. But I learned what her travels were about. When she spoke about going "home," she meant the concert halls where she once played. Perhaps once again she relived the bright yesterdays while standing in the eclipse of time. But did she think she could capture a shadow?

Over time, through sporadic glimpses, I came to see fragments of the person she had once been, passionate, intense, and free-spirited.

One day when I stopped to visit, I learned that she was gone.

"She walked out," I was told.

"How could she?" I cried. "This is a locked facility."

"It happens," the receptionist replied with indifference.

I never learned what happened to Helen. But often I think of her. Even though I was frightened for her, in my heart I hoped that she made it to New York.

One evening, after playing *Moonlight Sonata*, I sat down and penned a few words that I dedicated to her. These words are for you Helen, if you should ever stumble across this account.

Have you gone pursuing shadows?
They are not the best of you
Nor the ghost of you,
But relics of memory and desire.
Work and love and regrets
Are but shades of yesterday;
Helen, don't you know?
Sometimes twilight casts
The longest shadow?

PART II

Travels

Though we travel the world over
to find the beautiful,
to find the beautiful,
we must carry it with us,
or we find it not.

—RALPH WALDO EMERSON, "ART"

CHAPTER 8

A Funeral in China

I'VE ALWAYS AVOIDED ATTENDING funerals. In the general sense, I accept that they are for the living, not the dead. I can't see the logic of saying words of praise about a person who can no longer hear. In protest, I've been known to compose an elegy for a person in perfect health.

However, when my niece called and asked me to accompany her to China to attend a memorial service for her grandmother, I wholeheartedly said yes without giving it a second thought.

My niece, Xiaoman (pronounced *Sho-man*), came from China twenty years earlier to complete a doctorate in music composition. Here, she met and married my nephew. This would be her first trip back since coming to America.

Telling me about the service, she said, "My mother asked me to invite you. She's going back to her village to attend a ceremony for her mother, my grandmother. She hasn't been back to her home village for over fifty years."

I knew that Nia Nia (grandmother) had died while her three children were off fighting for the revolution during the 1940s. I asked Xiaoman, "Is it customary in China to have a memorial service so many years after a person's death?"

"This is a special situation, in honor of my mother, who couldn't be there when her mother died," she explained.

I'd met my niece's parents when they were visiting the United States years earlier. Yixia (*Yi-shia*), the father, is a royal descendant of the Han dynasty, an elegant man with regal bearing, and one of China's leading geologists. He is also a poet and a student of Chinese literature and calligraphy. Yueqing (*Yu-ching*), the mother, a soft-spoken, gentle woman who might be mistaken for an ordinary housewife, is a highly respected laser physicist.

Landing on Hainan Island, we were met by ten cars full of family and friends who would escort us to our palatial hotel. My driver, it turned out, was the city's chief of police. Others I met included Yueqing's brother, an architect of many five-star hotels throughout China and a codesigner of Tiananmen Square, and her sister who served as Mao's personal secretary. It was two in the morning when our caravan arrived at the hotel.

Swaying palms and a lively silvery ocean welcomed us to an exquisite setting. My room, as large as a hotel lobby, came beautifully appointed. A computer on the writing table was available free of charge to the guests. I logged on and picked up my messages. A frantic message from my husband appeared on the screen: "Where are you? Are you safe?" I replied, "I'm in the lap of God, surrounded by officials who seem committed to keeping me safe and well entertained." (And that never changed.) Wide French doors opened onto a balcony. I stepped into the balmy evening air and found myself in paradise. A

Chinese lantern-like moon shined down on a fragrant garden lining the balcony; the ocean sang below. Later as I drifted to sleep, I suddenly bolted upright. *Omigod, how much will this cost? It must be a thousand dollars a night!* I'd left the arrangements for the accommodations to my niece's parents. It turned out to be $35 per night—I was treated to the price charged to Chinese Communist party members.

The next morning, I found myself alone with Yueqing at the breakfast table. "Are you happy to return to the place of your childhood?" I asked.

A deliberate thinker, she reflected before answering. "Yes, good to see family. My cousins." She paused, struggling to translate her thoughts into English. "But so hard to see village. So hard."

"Hard?" I asked, puzzled.

"The memories. To see—the room."

Now, I am lost. But I wait patiently.

"You know I fight for Mao. A hard time. But I believe—we believe—we could have a better country. A great country. A country for the people." Her voice became thin and tight as she tried to hold back the anger. But I could hear it rising like the rumblings before an avalanche.

"But you are angry," I said.

"Yes. I gave everything. And they no decency to tell me. Not one whole year. I didn't know." She held up a finger to emphasize the one year.

Should I know this story? I wondered.

She rushed forward, words gushing out of her mouth like torrents of destructive water. "All of them. So frightened. Alone. All hanged herselves."

"What? Who?" I felt I'd been hit in the stomach. But she was not talking to me. She was telling the story for the first time aloud.

"My mother, my aunt, and my grandmother. My sister, my brother, me—we all run away to fight with Mao. They stay alone. Some people in village thought they had yuan, money; some accused them of property—no, how you say—landlord? They have nothing—just a house, nothing more. Poor like everyone. But some threatened them, called them capitalists. They alone. Three women. Afraid. No man to protect them. They hanged herselves, my mother, my grandmother, my aunt."

I could not speak, but one hand reached for her and the other went to my mouth to hold back a surprised sob. "Horrible." The word escaped when I found my breath.

Her voice trembled: "The next day they to be labeled 'most hated people,' a landlord, the country worst enemy. They scorned by whole village, by whole country. Why? They not know why. Her children away to fight for country. Who did this to them? We not know. All night they hugged each other and cried. Before the light, before the shame descended on them, they hanged herselves. All together. All alone."

Suddenly she finished, the anger and shame exhausted. She said quietly, "I not come back before. But now I am old. I come. I come to celebrate their life, to bury my anger."

We sat together in reverent silence for them. Finally, I spoke: "You honor me by asking me to share this with you."

She said, "I want to tell you. I glad you come. You family to us."

The next day we left the groomed paradise of our hotel grounds and drove into the countryside, a region of wretched poverty. Poverty is ungroomed, and it is filthy, and it stinks.

We traveled first to a small farming town large enough for a police station and a few shops. After a short stop at the police station to visit a cousin who was an officer, we drove from the town, traveling in a caravan down an unpaved road lined with tropical fruit trees, to the isolated, ancient walled village where Yueqing had grown up. We entered the compound through a resident's bedroom, such as it was: a pallet on the floor with a crumpled, tattered blanket next to it as though someone had made a hurried exit. Inside the walls, not one comfortable chair or couch was in sight. No children's toys were scattered about. There was no sign of dishes or glasses. An enormous black cauldron that was used to cook communal meals sat in the center courtyard, and nearby loomed a huge satellite dish. A large TV screen filled the community room where the villagers sat on the dirt floor to watch the government-filtered programs.

Yueqing paused before a doorway leading to a small house in the compound. Once inside, she made her way to a tiny room and stopped. Her body stiffened as she entered. I choked on the smell of ancient dusty stones, a thousand years old. A dim light sneaked though a small unglazed window high on the wall, covered by wax paper. I found it hard to breathe. Yueqing stood in the center of the room with tears running down her face. She was oblivious to the smell. She was alone with her memories. Feeling protective of her, I glared at the villagers who curiously crowded around the door to stare. But she was deep inside herself, unaware of them. Feeling awkward, I stood as sentinel by the door and tried to imagine what she saw. It was beyond my imagination.

The thick air and the heaviness of grief finally drove us outside. We then headed out of the compound, down a hill, across a meadow to a verdant knoll that looked across a heavily wooded valley and arrived at the cemetery. I recalled how anxious Yueqing had been about the gravesite, wondering whether it had been maintained, for it is shameful to neglect one's ancestors. Xiaoman confided to me that her father had secretly sent money ahead of this visit to pay someone to cut the grass and clean up around the headstone—to spare his wife shame. I stood apart from the others on a small incline above them and with relief could see a tidy gravesite. I watched as the ceremony below began.

The funeral commenced with each family member approaching the headstone, bowing in honor, and offering a prayer—words audible only to those standing close by. Yueqing stayed the longest, speaking softly, perhaps telling her deceased relatives all that had transpired since their deaths. She then reached for her daughter and introduced Xiaoman to her grandmother, great-grandmother, and great-aunt. Xiaoman honored them with words of respect. When these rituals ended, the mood shifted suddenly to one of a happy celebration. The cousin, who worked for the nearby police department, passed out items from a large plastic bag. Then cousins and tagalongs lit firecrackers amid shouts of laughter. Paper money was set on fire; this was money meant for the dead to spend along their journey in the afterlife. Favorite foods and candies were also placed before the headstone for the dead to later enjoy.

When the celebration wound down, Yueqing waved me over. Standing next to Yueqing before the simple headstone, I asked her what the inscription said. She read, "The property of Mr....," and said a man's name that I can't remember. Deceased women had no individual identity but were remembered only in relation to the man who "possessed" them. The women were deemed the "property" of Nia Nia's husband, who had died a few years before them. All three women were buried in the same grave—or so I thought, until my niece whispered in my ear that there were no bodies in the grave. The women's bodies had been dumped into the river after they were found hanged by the villagers. *Maybe even by some of the ones who had greeted us so warmly when we entered the compound,* I thought.

I walked away from the celebration and sat on a large rock. As I looked across the serene valley, I thought of the three women, two only in their forties, caught in the vortex of political terror. Three women, alone and frightened, unable to endure the shame of ridicule and banishment. Three women who would never realize the accomplishments of their offspring who fought for a better life, a better country. The memory of that black night faded into a warm summer afternoon where laughter rang out in place of tears. The women had been reinstated into grace, allowed a place to be buried because of the accomplishments of their heirs—a hollow compensation!

After the ceremony, a luncheon in honor of our visit had been arranged by the mayor of the town, a young woman who had been recently voted into office. (Some areas in China are experimenting with a modified form of democracy.) A large room above a restaurant was crowded with family members, as well as some who claimed to be; but nobody was turned away from the festivities and a free meal. Among them was a toothless man in his nineties who kept grinning and bowing to me. No one in the group knew who he was.

I was seated next to Yueqing at the head of the table, a place of honor, and the mayor asked me to give a greeting from America. I told her that it would be a privilege to do so. The outside temperature was near 100 degrees, the room was even hotter, and at the place of honor sat a giant bowl of steaming soup perched on top of a small burner. Its vapor drifted toward me and drenched me in its mist; I was trapped in a sauna and felt faint from the heat. Dripping with perspiration, I rose and greeted the attentive audience. Many had never met an American. Xiaoman was my translator, and the people laughed with delight when I told them how fascinated Americans were with Chinese culture. Knowing they referred to Americans as "the white devils," I explained that I hoped I'd be seen as a "white friend." Many were eager to touch my hair and clothes, and my heart filled with friendliness and respect for them.

Following the meal, the mayor accompanied us on a visit to a local elementary school. When I saw how pathetically destitute the children were, I felt ashamed of the small gifts of candy and silly plastic toys I had brought for them. How in need they were of basic supplies such as crayons and writing paper! The dilapidated school building, with broken doors and missing windows, and sparsely furnished classroom tore at me. But the children's spirits were buoyant. Before we left, Xiaoman, her parents, several others, and I committed to purchasing a computer, a tape player, and other audio-visual equipment for the school. Tears of gratitude filled the principal's eyes. He told us that the parents must pay for the children's workbooks, and the parents in this province could not afford even the small amount required. Such equipment would greatly advance their learning.

Though this was a trip in memoriam, it was also most memorable. The extravagance and extremes within the country are fixed in my memory. The opulence and grandeur of the resort versus the stark, meager livelihoods beyond its walls are irreconcilable in my mind. But despite the poverty, everywhere I traveled, I was met with friendly generosity.

I am also grateful for what I learned about myself during this trip. The truth about my aversion to funerals is not about the words said for those who can no longer hear but about my discomfort with expressing heart-wrenching grief in front of others. I lost that discomfort. Grief is about love. Whether for the living or for the deceased, poet Elizabeth Barrett Browning's words resound:

> I love thee with the breath,
> Smiles, tears, of all my life; and, if God choose,
> I shall but love thee better after death.

CHAPTER 9

Saved by a Coup

I WAS BROUGHT UP to always tell the truth, to obey the law, and to follow the Ten Commandments. Sadly, I have failed in each category. However, I plead innocent to breaking the law that could have landed me inside a Thai prison. It's because of people like me that we are subjected to the tedious drone of airport announcements warning us "Do not transport any objects from a person you do not know."

My husband joined a group of male friends to sail the Finnish fjords. So, while he was away, I teamed up with Barbara, a newly divorced travel agent friend, to tour Hong Kong, Malaysia, Singapore, and Thailand. Our first stop was Hong Kong. In the lobby of the Mandarin Hotel, an attractive man invited us to a party in the penthouse suite. Attending were representatives from the great houses of clothing designers. Barbara straightaway met a handsome Brazilian banker. Looking around, I recognized the captain of our flight, a few passengers, and our exquisite guide, Suzy. She looked stunning in her red silk Mandarin dress with a side slit cut nearly to her waist. Catching my eye, she glided over.

"I'm coming down with a cold. I can't make the next leg to Thailand. Could you do me a favor? I've an envelope that I promised a friend. Would you mind taking it for me?" Although she asked, her voice carried an "of course you will" tone.

You see, I felt I owed her one. I had arrived at Los Angeles International Airport having left my medical documentation on my bedside table. It contained certification that I'd had the vaccinations required by some of the countries I would be visiting.

"Not a problem," Suzy said as she hurried me into the bathroom. She pulled from her purse a stamp and a blank form. "You have had the required vaccinations?" she asked, nodding her head.

"Of course," I told her honestly. But I couldn't remember the address of the health clinic that gave them.

She waved it off lightly. "We'll just make one up. Give me a name of a street in your city." She began to write, and after filling in each required vaccination, she stamped it with an official medical stamp.

My eyes grew wide. *Is this legal?* I didn't dare ask how she had gotten the stamp.

"This happens all the time, people forgetting to bring the document," she assured me. And as easy as that, I was in compliance and able to enter the countries.

"Do you do passports, too, when someone's forgotten theirs?" I asked half-jokingly.

She laughed and shook her head. Suzy was so beautiful, I doubted anyone would think her capable of such stealth.

So, eager to set the relationship in balance, I accepted the large, heavy envelope she handed me at the party.

The day of our departure, Suzy saw us off and gave me final instructions. "Your guide will take you to a restaurant tonight for dinner and a show. A waiter will approach and will ask, 'How was your stay in Hong Kong?' You will know that he is the one to give the envelope. Don't be obvious; put it on the table, under the menu, and he'll pick it up when he takes the menu from you."

"What's in it?" I asked timidly, as if it was none of my business.

"Some magazines. It's for a female in the royal family. Magazines that are hard to come by in Thailand. Don't worry about it." Her calm voice implied the matter was trivial.

Still, I was a bit worried. On the plane, I told Barbara about the package. "Most likely it's *Playgirl* magazines. I bet those girls have some wild slumber parties," Barbara said with an exuberant laugh. She explained to me that *Playgirl* was a new magazine that was for girls what *Playboy* was for boys. Her high-spirited laughter put my fears to rest.

I don't judge others for their reading habits, but I did start to get nervous when the stewardess made an announcement just before landing: "We are arriving in Thailand, a country that delivers severe penalties for contraband. I recommend that anyone carrying drugs without a prescription label on the bottle visit the lavatory and deposit it there. Leave any other contraband on the plane. If you don't, you run the risk of not seeing your country again."

A line quickly formed at the bathroom door. I whispered to my well-traveled friend, "Do you think the magazines are legal here?" She laughed and said she didn't think so. The acrid taste of panic rose in my throat. What should I do about the envelope? It was in my checked bag and not to be seen until I stood before a customs official.

I'm not a good liar; in fact, I'm downright lousy. My face turns red and my eyes behave like Mexican jumping beans. Ahead, a stern officer awaited my papers. My legs turned to rubber and my heart began to boom like an Asian temple drum. I feared my heart betrayed me and exposed my crime. Not only was I carrying contraband, but I also had a forged medical certificate. I began to visualize that I might never see my country again.

Cacophony erupted as swarms of individuals carrying cameras and microphones charged into the area. Their expectant faces scanned the passengers. Clearly, they anticipated someone newsworthy. *Oh, no. I've been found out. They've come to televise my arrest.* Then I saw them point and someone shouted, "There he is." I nearly collapsed with relief when I heard that on our plane was a former leader who had been exiled was returning home to die. They were there for him!

Suddenly the crowd scattered. Soldiers ran through the terminal carrying weapons with bayonets, dangerously stabbing at the air. Gunfire exploded nearby.

A police official appeared from nowhere and waved our group toward the exit, bypassing the inspection officer. "Americans. Over here! Outside! Hurry!" he shouted. Holding tight to my uninspected possessions, I ran toward the exit. We scrambled inside a waiting bus with open doors. The bus driver gunned the engine, turned away from the mobs and gunfire, and drove us safely to our hotel. I had dodged a bullet.

The nightly news reported that the expatriate's arrival had triggered a coup. I was saved by a coup!

The noise and bustle of Bangkok made it impossible to hold on to one's thoughts. Just as well—its exotic sights and smells would overpower you if the racket didn't. The cigarette boats that sped through the canals, selling produce and transporting passengers, left me mesmerized. The wild ride on a tuk-tuk motorcycle taxi, careening around food kiosks, nearly took my breath away. The kaleidoscopic beauty of the exotic Temple of Dawn nearly blinded me as the rays of sunlight bounced off the porcelain fragments of shattered teacups and saucers that decorated the temple. I stood in awe before the giant Jade Buddha, located at Wat Phra Kaew on the grounds of the king's Grand Palace.

After sightseeing, we were taken back to the hotel for dinner and entertainment as promised. I discreetly placed the envelope beneath my menu. A tall, handsome male appeared. He asked how we liked our stay in Hong Kong, the expected clue, and I subtly moved my menu so that he could see the envelope. He pretended interest in taking our order, but after securing the envelope, he turned the matter of ordering over to a young female waitress and he disappeared.

As we were leaving the dining room, he reappeared. Artfully moving us aside, away from the other travelers, he said quietly, "My lady is grateful to you." Then he surprised me with, "She would like to send her limousine tomorrow and have her personal astrologer give you and your friend a private reading." He nodded toward Barbara.

"But what about the coup?" I asked. "Is the royal family safe?"

He smiled, patient with my naïveté about their politics. "Oh, they are in no danger. The people love the family. Coups are the people's way of restructuring the parliament."

Interesting concept, I thought.

The next morning, a driver in a Rolls-Royce picked us up at the hotel and drove us to a lovely estate with manicured gardens located in the country. The only information we provided our astrologer was our date of birth. She read our palms and then the tea leaves we left in our cups after drinking delectable jasmine tea. Now, it wasn't a mystery how she managed to predict that Barbara would meet a dark, handsome Brazilian. For, indeed, Barbara had not returned to our hotel room the night before. And the handsome Brazilian we'd met at the party in Hong Kong had traveled with us to Thailand. The seer warned Barbara, however, to guard her heart from this Romeo. I could have told her that!

But how did she manage to name the three fruit trees in my backyard? My husband had taken a job in another county, and we planned to move as soon as we both returned home. Who informed her that my house was up for sale? She foretold that it wouldn't sell for many years. She predicted that I would achieve the highest degree in my line of study, and only after I retired would I move from the area where I was living. She took my hand and held it tenderly and, looking deep into my eyes, said, "I don't want to alarm you, but your husband, who is now over water, will pass on before you. I see he is much older than you, my dear. So, live your days with him in happiness. And there will be many." How did she know these things, that he was over water, that there was an age difference between us? I suppose when one is connected to the powerful, one can find out anything. Still, all I can say is that everything she forecasted came to pass.

When we arrived back in Hong Kong, I asked Suzy what had been in the envelope. Barbara had guessed right. "The girls love those magazines," she explained.

I said, "But if they had found them on me, I could have gone to prison."

With a carefree laugh, she said, "Oh, someone would have gotten you out."

I wondered how Suzy learned about what the royal women enjoyed reading. Maybe it was the same way the astrologer learned her information. I must admit that I have often wondered about the astrologer's perspicacity, even though her reading didn't convert me to a believer. And I don't believe that I would ever make an accomplished smuggler or spy or liar. So, I've come to accept the caveat of the airlines: don't carry packages from a stranger. Next time, I might not be saved by a coup!

CHAPTER 10

Ghosts and Crosses

AH, SINGAPORE, A SHANGRI-LA of parks and serene gardens and a unique blend of old and new. Among other tourist attractions, it is known for "Boogie Street," a place of open-air restaurants and Billy-boys, slender boys who parade the street dressed as delicate and beautiful females. Imagine my surprise when I witnessed a "woman" at the urinal when I entered the common bathroom. The small island became independent as the Republic of Singapore in 1965. Although the government is tolerant of the Billy-boys, it rules with an iron fist. People can be heavily fined or jailed if they carelessly toss a cigarette on the streets.

It is also a country of sudden squalls—and ghosts. And it's home to the over one-hundred-year-old Raffles Hotel, named in honor of Stamford Raffles, the British governor who founded modern Singapore in the early nineteenth century. The hotel is a place renowned for attracting writers who went there for inspiration, including Joseph Conrad, Rudyard

Kipling, Noel Coward, and W. Somerset Maugham, who called it the symbol of "all the fables of the Exotic East."

As I was waiting for dinner in the garden at the hotel, the umbrellas suddenly started to echo like clapping hands, introducing lightning and wind. Before I could gather my belongings, sheets of rain came from over the sea. I ran for the famous Long Bar in the hotel; the room was alive with excitement about the storm, and strangers were mixing as though they were old friends. The high ceiling fans purred, and their murmur assured us they had seen such tempests countless times. I felt exuberant, knowing I was in the same place that so many great writers had gathered, and yet alone at the same time as I watched the high-spirited strangers make frivolous connections. Someone in the bar disclosed the rumor that ghosts roamed the halls, especially near the rooms where the writers once slept. One too many Singapore Slings later, I went in search of inspiration, hoping to encounter one of the ghosts. Down the corridor called "The 12 Personality Suites," I stopped in front of a door with a plaque dedicated to W. Somerset Maugham. Sliding to the floor, I leaned against the wall, wishing that somehow Maugham's genius would be transmitted to me. I felt drawn to him more than to the other visiting writers who had frequented the hotel. Since reading his work, I wanted to sit at his feet and glean wisdom from his great philosophical and cultured mind. Suddenly, he loomed above me.

"Why have you summoned me?" he growled.

Caught off guard by his sudden appearance, I tried to find my voice.

"Well, go on. Get it over with. You want to ask me about *Of Human Bondage*? That's why most people come." It was Maugham all right—he still stammered.

"Was it autobiographical?" I asked, knowing the question was controversial.

"Not again. How many times do I have to say it, some of it was autobiographical, but it was *fiction*."

"That's what I want to write, narrative fiction," I said, hoping he would offer some free advice. "I've been told that one should only write about what one knows. But I've read somewhere that you stole stories. Someone tells you something personal about their life and then that story appears in one of your plays or books."

He sighed with boredom. "Every writer is a thief. After exhausting bits from his own life, the writer will seize upon any scene, event, or person that stimulates his imagination and will weave it into his writing. Sadly, however, I have been libeled by women who say I stayed with them and then abused their hospitality by ridiculing them in my writings—creatures so vain and with lives so drab they readily identified themselves in exchange for some trivial infamy. I'd never even met them," he said with a schooled imperious inflection. Then with a brusque apology, he added, "As I have written, fact and fiction are so intermingled in my work that now, looking back on it, I can hardly distinguish one from the other."

"Yes, I remember you said something like that in *The Summing Up*."

"Well, if you've read it, why have you come? If you think I'm looking for a story, I'm finished with writing. Are you here to tell me your story, and is it worth telling?"

I gave the question serious consideration and I drew in a deep breath, "Well," I began in all seriousness, fully intending to lay out my life for him. Then I saw him glance at his watch and I changed my mind. I really wanted to ask him about writing, but since I'd already read his thoughts about it in *The Summing Up*, I instead asked, "Have you seen the others, Kipling and Conrad? Is there a heaven just for writers?"

"I can't answer that. We haven't been able to extricate ourselves from here. Too many people like you come seeking us out, haunting us."

"I thought that's what you did," I said shyly, suppressing a giggle.

"You are wrong, dead wrong. Ghosts want to be left alone. I tell you, it is people who seek them out—contrary to popular conjecture," he growled.

"Oh, I see," I replied, sounding sympathetic. Then fearful I had annoyed him and that he might turn away, I rushed to ask the question really on my mind: "Do you have any words of wisdom to offer someone—about writing?"

"Ah, just as I thought!" he said. "Why? Do you have anything to say that hasn't already been said?" he asked.

Had he read my mind? Why did one write? In an inarticulate way, I tried to explain to him my reason: "I just want to tell stories. Stories can help people know they're not alone in their human struggles." I fell silent as I wrestled with the purpose of it. "I'm not even sure I can write, and I'm confused with the reasons for it. I just want to do it."

"Hmm," he said thoughtfully, "I've said everything I can about it in the book you referenced. If you remember, I told how no one taught me to write. I struggled to teach myself. The most important advice I'll give is to write with lucidity." I thought he was finished. Then he added, "And don't write to become famous. People are merciless and they'll keep after you, even after you've earned the right to peace and silence. And if you think it will make you immortal, you've been misled.

Who reads Laurence Sterne or Thomas Hardy? Within a few generations, one is forgotten." He reached over and placed a hand on my shoulder to emphasize his words.

I could see him fading—just the thinnest silhouette of him remained. Before disappearing, he turned and said the strangest thing: "The greatest tragedy of life is not that men perish, but that they cease to love." I called out to him, reaching for his fading image. I wanted to hear more.

Suddenly I was staring up into a lovely Asian face. Maugham was gone. The maid anxiously and gently was shaking me. Seeing that I was conscious, she asked if she could help me to my room.

Singapore will always hold a revered place in my heart because of my brief conversation with a ghost. Though I hoped he'd say more about writing, as he informed me, he said it all in *The Summing Up*.

I left Singapore in a typhoon. During the flight, the door of the cockpit flew open and the soft glow from the cockpit's interior light made it seem as if the Jade Buddha from the temple in Thailand was in charge. The portly pilot wrestled with the volatile plane, which tumbled as whimsically as a leaf in the wind.

Grateful for a safe landing in Hong Kong, I thought it was fitting to visit the thirty-four-meter-high Big Buddha near the Po Lin Monastery on Lantau Island, an hour's ferry ride from Hong Kong. I wished to toss flowers at the Buddha's feet and give thanks for having survived the three weeks of travel through Southeast Asia.

However, the word *monastery* landed me in trouble. The ferry weaved its way through tiny islands, making several stops before arriving at Lantau. My traveling friend Barbara assigned me the role of guide as she had collapsed into a state of misery after her Brazilian suitor said goodbye in Thailand. I checked at each stop with a crew member to make sure we didn't get off at the wrong place. The last crew member that I consulted didn't speak English, so I used the charade gesture of a cross to indicate my destination. He nodded and pointed to a hill in the distance, and sure enough, a large cross dominated the mountaintop. Barbara turned skeptical when she noted that we were the only tourists to exit the boat among villagers who were herding pigs and carrying cages of chickens and baskets loaded with produce.

We climbed our way up the steep incline until we came to the monastery. We found ourselves among several buildings with crosses on top. The large cross we'd seen from the boat loomed in the distance. We found no Big Buddha. Inside one of the buildings we asked about the Buddha, but the priest placed his fingers over his lips to indicate silence. In fact, everyone used the same gesture with us. Outside, I consulted my guidebook. I collapsed on the ground in laughter when I realized my stupidity: Buddhists don't display crosses! (I confess, I've never been good at charades; a big-bellied gesture might have been better.) Instead of arriving at the famous Po Lin Monastery, we found ourselves at a Trappist monastery with a cadre of priests who had taken a vow of silence. We had gotten off on the wrong side of the island!

Now what? Hot and tired, we made our way back to the spot where the ferry had dropped us off. The guidebook indicated that the ferry stopped at this site only once a day. How would we get back to Hong Kong? In the distance we spotted a sampan propelled by a small outboard motor. We waved in desperation and called out frantically to the driver. A slender boy who looked no older than twelve greeted us. For a fee, he agreed to take us across the water to catch the ferry returning to Hong Kong. His passengers, local islanders, crowded together to make room for us, some having to sit atop their cages of squawking birds and squealing pigs. But as soon as we were midway between the island and the ferry to Hong Kong, the motor died. We were stranded in the middle of the sea, far from either destination. The young boy didn't seem worried; he slipped out of his clothes and jumped overboard. His small smiling face resurfaced. Using gestures, he assured us he could fix the problem.

The sun grew hotter, the animals became restless, and my mouth got dry from thirst and worry. If we missed the ferry, we'd also miss our flight home. Finally, the engine restarted. Then within a short distance, it stopped again. In fact, the engine hiccupped its way forward, stopping and causing the boy to repeat his heroic efforts. After each success, the boy was met with applause by the passengers. We kept pointing anxiously to our watches and to the ferry in the distance as it made its way into the distant harbor. The boy was not to be rushed. His priority was to drop off his passengers at their planned stops. After the last passenger was safely landed, he threw the engine into full throttle and we shot off like a small missile riding high on the water. With two minutes to spare, he maneuvered the small craft skillfully next to the enormous ferry. We paid him a handsome fee, and then we darted up the gangplank, ebullient.

Although I didn't get to thank Buddha for his protection and the great experiences on this journey, I learned from the Dhammapada, his doctrine, which says, "All that is is the result of what we have thought." My thoughts have given thanks, and that is enough.

I have returned to these cities on other occasions, but there is nothing like seeing them for the first time. The brain has a way of rapidly turning the extraordinary into the familiar. Memory, on the other hand, saves us from that fate. However, I also remember what W. Somerset Maugham conveyed to me at the Raffles Hotel: fact and fiction sometimes become so entangled that it's hard to separate them.

CHAPTER 11

Shipwrecked in Strasbourg

BOUFFON WAS THE ONLY word I recognized amid the torrent of French words spewing from our boat's skipper as he screamed at the crew who had come to rescue us. Each time he said it, he punctuated the word with a raised middle finger. Then he turned to me, yelling in English to drop the stern anchor. Unsure of where it was, I yanked a line wrapped around the bollard in the area he pointed, freeing it from the cleat, and watched as the anchor disappeared into the water. Relieved, I heard the clank of the chain follow and felt the boat lurch as it came to a stop.

David, my husband, ran forward to free the bow anchor, but it was too late. The boat made a wide arc and slammed against an ancient stone bridge spanning the River Ill, blocking the public waterway. Dreading the worst, we stared in disbelief. Our captain, Victor, bolted below. "No water leak, not yet!" he announced as his head surfaced. He slumped onto the bulkhead in exasperation and rubbed his white hair between his fingers. He then jumped to his feet to lambaste the tug pilot, but he was out of earshot.

Nevertheless, the title *bouffon* was indeed earned. Victor, an American doctor, had mastered the French language as a student of medicine in Paris many, many years earlier. Now, as a respite from his busy practice, he went sailing on his boat, which he left anchored in foreign ports until his return. On this venture, David, I, and Alice, Victor's companion, were on board.

Earlier we had turned from the French canal system onto the River Ill, which encircles the city of Strasbourg. Our destination: *le port ancien*, the ancient port of the city. *A marina! Hot showers! Cold drinks!* For weeks we had been motoring through the verdant French countryside, tying up along the banks of the Moselle and French canals. Having left Luxembourg nearly a month earlier, we planned to end our journey in Marseille. How I had looked forward to a return to civilization in Strasbourg. How eager I was to see the great cathedral with its grand fourteenth-century astronomical clock. But I was even more eager for a long, hot shower.

We stared in wonder at the beauty of Strasbourg, known as the petite Paris, as we slowly made our way up the river, looking for the port identified on our navigation chart. Our boat was a beautiful double-ender forty-three-foot Hans Christian cutter. The stepped mast lay lengthwise across the top cabin; an American flag hung from a pole on the stern. By the time we passed under the third bridge spanning the river, we realized that we must have passed the port.

We had been moving upstream against a mild flow. Suddenly we found ourselves buffeted by a powerful current. We could not turn to go back downstream; we would have been moving too fast with little or no steering control in the swift water. The skipper had us drop the bow anchor to secure us and radioed the port authority for assistance.

After a short delay, a small tow vessel with a single operator appeared. In French, Victor instructed the pilot of the tow vessel to take a strong line from our stern, and then let us raise our bow anchor and slowly reverse the direction of our boat. With the line, he was to hold us against the current with his motor and very slowly control our downstream travel, back under the stone bridge we had just passed and into the wider bay below it that we now knew contained *le port ancien*, which turned out to be nothing more than a place to throw a line and tie up on a main busy thoroughfare of shops and shoppers.

Victor insisted that the pilot repeat his instructions so there would be no misunderstanding. All went well as we were slowly turned. Then to our horror, the pilot blithely threw off the line! The dangling line caught around our prop, killing the engine. We were at the mercy of the powerful current. That's when our skipper, Victor, bellowed "Bouffon!" with instructions to me to drop the stern anchor.

This was the beginning of our troubles. Soon a voice blaring from a bullhorn demanded that we move our vessel, which was blocking the passage of a large tourist dinner boat. Victor rose to his full six-foot-two height and, looking like a wrathful Moses with his flowing white hair, shouted back in French, "This is the fault of your buffoon, and I'm not moving an inch until Lloyd's of London arrives and tells me what damage we have."

It was five o'clock on a warm June day. The banks along the Ill began to fill with bystanders on their way home from work. Five o'clock was also the hour when the lock to the Rhine

River was opened to release water into the River Ill, raising its level to accommodate the draft of the large tourist boats. This release, the sudden surge of water, precipitated our crisis. I looked beyond the bridge and saw two cruise boats waiting and behind them a string of small boats whose passengers planned to dine in one of the charming restaurants along the canal.

Shortly, a *petit bateau*, a craft not much larger than a rowboat, with an outboard appeared with three men in uniforms. They were officials with the port authority, and they ordered us to move our boat. Victor was unmovable. The conversation escalated from an order to an argument. The authorities explained that the city loses revenue if the tourist boats cannot proceed. But Victor remained intractable. He was determined to wait for an insurance adjustor. He was certain there was damage because we had heard the boat bottom scrape rock and then heard a loud snap as the boat swung into the bridge.

The crowd began to enjoy the melee. Hearing voices calling to us, I looked overhead and saw two young people leaning over the bridge, happily lowering two bottles of wine tied to a rope. As though the situation were up for vote, the crowd was keeping score of the argument with loud boos or yeas. I was relieved that we had some allies.

Two more boats appeared, one from the fire department, the other from the gendarmerie, the police department. The firemen gallantly ordered the rescue of the female passengers, that being me and Alice, the skipper's beautiful companion. Just before Alice and I boarded the firemen's small unseaworthy-looking vessel, Victor handed me the telephone number of his office in Los Angeles with orders to his secretary to have Lloyd's of London send an appraiser to the site, pronto!

The two men sent to rescue us wore the only available life jackets. The outboard engine coughed and died several times before starting, but when we arrived in midstream it quit, and the boat swirled in the eddy, tipping and bobbing like a cork, and we hung on for dear life. We landed with a thump on the riverbank.

A young man approached and told us that he was an American medical student studying at the university. Along with others, he had been observing the drama in the river. He took us straightaway to his apartment nearby and generously let me use his telephone. I was able to talk with Victor's secretary, who assured me she would immediately contact the insurance company in London. Our host then offered us a cool drink and a place to freshen up.

Alice and I made our way back to the area of our marooned boat, but there was no boat when we arrived. The crowd had disappeared and boat traffic along the river and under the bridges had resumed. Where were Victor and David? Where had the boat been taken?

I approached a policeman standing on the bridge and in faltering French asked, "Ou est le petit bateau?" With the help of a bystander, we gleaned that the port authority had boarded our boat, moved it, and then secured it between two locks near the city hospital, where it had been placed under "port arrest."

"Your boat is a criminal and won't be released until it pays a fine," the policeman informed us in an imperious voice.

"A criminal?" I asked disbelievingly.

"Yes, it damaged our bridge!"

This was a bridge securely standing after having been bombed in two major wars.

Alice's wide-eyed expression conveyed that she expected that we, too, would be taken into custody. But I knew with her head-turning beauty, she would inspire rescue, not retribution. As we headed to where the boat had been impounded, we met David and Victor, who had come in search of us.

Our mooring turned out to be in an unsavory section of the city, a smelly backyard where the hospital deposited its refuse, a place where transients made their home. The lockkeeper had been instructed to notify authorities if we attempted an escape. Victor notified the American consulate of our problem and made an appointment for the next day. Trapped, tired, and hungry, we could do little else but wait—and have dinner. The lockkeeper was a good sort of fellow and recommended the city's finest restaurant, where we could celebrate Victor's birthday.

Strasbourg had double daylight saving time. At ten thirty that evening, we were dining at the top of the city's tallest building, mesmerized by the magnificent vista enhanced by a brilliant red sunset, and imbibing a glass of wine as richly colored as our sky. We lifted our glasses in a toast to our skipper and to Strasbourg and gave in to the effects of the wine and matchless food.

We arrived back at the boat in high spirits, laughing at the details of our day's adventure. Lloyd's of London would be arriving in the morning. The American consulate would intercede. All would be well.

Before retiring, we settled bills incurred from my grocery shopping over the past week. I had signed on to be the chef on this journey, so I oversaw meal planning, and our arrangement was to split the cost of groceries. Since we had not been near a bank for several weeks, I had accumulated quite a sum of cash. I stuffed the money in my purse and hid it above my bunk, then climbed into bed. Happy to be alone at last with my thoughts, I pulled the sheet over my face, hoping to lessen the dank, pungent smell of the river.

I lay awake wondering about the wisdom of this change in our lives. My husband and I had sold our busy psychiatric practice to take a lengthy sabbatical. We signed on as crew of this boat, which Victor planned to charter once it arrived in the Mediterranean. My job was chef; David's was deck hand. This was to be a trial run for circumnavigation in our own boat. When I was not preparing meals, I helped David on deck with the opening and closing of locks. It was backbreaking work, which required scrambling up ladders and manually opening four heavy metal doors, necessary for entering and leaving a lock. *Am I cut out for this sort of life?* I wondered.

I missed the calm, gracious setting of my office. I missed the daily routine and the predictable problems my clients brought.

Water could be so unpredictable! I was not a swimmer and had learned over time that Poseidon, the Greek god of the sea, had something against me. Lying in the boat's bunk, I comforted myself with the knowledge that we were Americans and our embassy would take care of us. *Tomorrow will be a better day*, I sighed to myself as I slipped into sleep.

Little did I know.

I woke the next morning to the noisy chirping of a robin perched on the open hatch. What a fuss he was making! My hand fumbled along the overhead ledge until I found my watch—six o'clock. I listened for the sounds of human stirring. The cabin resonated with only the deep rhythm of sleep.

Gradually, I heard the sounds of a city awakening: a whining truck collecting trash, the optimistic ring of church chimes, the stop and start of cars. Ah, yes, Strasbourg, France. Yesterday's happenings flooded back.

Slipping out of bed to peer outside, I saw the outline of the city hospital silhouetted against a sky that promised rain. After closing the hatch, I crawled back into bed. *That's funny*, I mused. *Why was the hatch open?* Someone must have gotten up during the night. Victor, our skipper, usually secured the boat before retiring, but so much happened yesterday, maybe he forgot.

Try as I might, I could not fall asleep again, so I rose and made coffee. The most important part of my role as chef was to brew coffee that could wake the dead. The aroma acted like an alarm clock and soon Victor, Alice, and David appeared in the salon.

Over coffee we planned the day's schedule. First, we would fetch fuel. Due to a gasoline shortage in Europe, boats could not be fueled at the docks. David, Victor, and Alice would transport the diesel fuel in large plastic containers. I would stay to guard the boat, make breakfast, and greet the appraiser from Lloyd's of London, whom we hoped would arrive by nine o'clock. When the officials had moved the boat under our protest, Victor discovered the steering quadrant, which controls the rudder, had been broken. The appraiser would recommend a shipyard where it could be repaired. The next item was to keep our ten o'clock appointment with the American consulate. The officials would, of course, end this ridiculous joke of arresting a boat.

While the crew went off for fuel, I seized the moment to shower and groom myself. My purse, which contained my only hairbrush and a meager supply of cosmetics, was not where I had last placed it—on the ledge above my bunk. Maybe David had moved it. Or maybe I hadn't put it above the bunk. Maybe it had fallen and someone placed it elsewhere. Calmly, I searched the obvious places. No purse. A panic began to swell. It had to be here. It contained a large sum of money, my passport, and three credit cards. Disbelief caused me to search in unusual places: in the refrigerator, beneath the settee, in the microwave. I couldn't bring myself to think the worst. I halfway expected to see my husband with it over his shoulder when he arrived back at the boat.

But when he returned, he carried only the fuel containers. David opened the hatch to call down to me. Suddenly I understood why I had found the hatch open. All a burglar had to do was put an arm through the hatch and lift my purse off the ledge where I had placed it the night before.

"We've been robbed," I screamed.

When Mr. Remy, the surveyor with Lloyd's of London, arrived at the boat, David and I were away telephoning the States to cancel my credit cards. Mr. Remy gave us the name of a first-rate shipyard where we could get repairs done. It was across the border in Germany, on the Rhine, near the entrance to the Black Forest.

At ten o'clock sharp we arrived at 15 Avenue D'Alsace, the American consulate. The consul was late. Finally, we were ushered into the office, where we were met by an assistant to an assistant of the appointed consul. He was exactly how Hollywood would cast a diplomat, a Cary Grant type—tall, immaculately groomed, slightly arrogant, and oh so confident.

"I'm sorry for keeping you waiting. But this DC-10 crisis has us all tied up in meetings."

We nodded in sympathy. David and I were on the plane leaving for Europe to join Victor just ahead of American Airlines Flight 191, which crashed as it left O'Hare airport on May 25, 1979. On landing, we learned of the crash and heard that 258 passengers perished, as well as 13 crew members and 2 people on the ground. All DC-10s had been grounded. We were surprised when the consul informed us that the investigation was being held in Strasbourg. The problem with sailing is that the only interest one has in news is the weather.

We explained how we came to be detained by the port authority and how we needed to leave the country, for a shipyard in Germany, to get the boat repaired.

"Yes, I saw the story in the paper." He unfolded the tidy newspaper on the desk and passed it to Victor.

Victor broke into loud laughter. "Listen to this." He turned to us, and read the account of how at five o'clock, an American vessel arrived on the River Ill under full sail and struck a bridge, causing it extensive damage. "How can they print this drivel? Our mast was stepped, lying across the deck, and there was not a breath of wind anywhere. We didn't even leave a dent in the bridge."

The assistant to the assistant consul gave a wry smile and said, "Not to worry. I know the head of the port authority personally. One phone call and you'll be on your way." He was dialing the phone as he spoke.

We could hear his end of the conversation and could tell it wasn't going well. When he hung up, he said, "You're free to go, but first you must pay a fine of $50,000." It was the same sum that Victor had threatened to sue if officials damaged his boat while moving it.

More phone calls were made but without success. Our American intermediary remained cool, assuring us, "We'll get this straightened out. Don't worry." I told him about the robbery and my missing passport. Eager to be helpful, he offered to reissue me a new one. He arranged an appointment for me at a place where I could be photographed as he filled out the necessary papers. He assured us that he would bring the boat matter to the attention of the consul as soon as he was free and someone from their office would be in touch.

After walking several blocks in pouring rain to the photography studio, I arrived wet and bedraggled. My bad mood and unkempt appearance were captured in the new passport photo. The saying goes, when you start looking like your passport photo, it's time to return home. But I was more worried that the unflattering photo might raise some official's suspicion about my affiliation with a terrorist organization.

The next day, however, events brightened. An employee from the consulate's office arrived with my purse, including the credit cards and the old passport, which had now been canceled. It was minus only the cash and the hairbrush. The considerate burglar had tossed the purse over the consulate's fence. Since he kept the hairbrush, I wondered if he was a "long-haired cat burglar."

We were informed that we were free to leave the area but the boat was not. David and I left Victor and Alice and went to retrieve our rented Citroen, which we had left at a secure location. Our routine was that after anchoring at the day's end, we'd return for the car and use it for sightseeing around the area the following day. The next few days while waiting for our boat's release, we visited the sites of Strasbourg, including the Petite France and the grand cathedral; the towns of Baden-

Baden, Riquewihr, and Colmar; and the vineyards at Bergheim where we purchased two cases of wine from the J. J. Müller vineyards.

A few days later when we returned to the boat from one of our adventures, there was a scribbled note on the door that said we were free to leave the city if we paid a fine of 1,000 French francs. The "fine" was the fee for moving the boat during our "distress." The currency conversion at that time brought the amount to approximately $50 US, so we agreed.

For another $150, we managed to hire a boat to tow us through the locks, onto the Rhine River, and to a beautiful shipyard in Freistett, a lovely marina at the edge of the Black Forest. As we entered the slip where the boat would be lifted out of the water to repair its damage, the pilot put the boat into reverse and the prop fell off into the water. Apparently, the frogman who had been sent underwater to release the rope that caught around our prop had dropped the nut holding the prop. So, when the engine was put into reverse at Freistett marina, the prop unscrewed itself and fell into the water. Thank goodness it happened when we were in a harbor and not on the open Rhine.

While the boat was being towed, I drove the car across the border planning to meet the boat at the marina in Germany. Unbeknownst to me, there had been a shooting at the crossing the day before. Merrily I handed the border guard my week-old passport with the photo that bore a resemblance to a terrorist. The German officer held my passport, noting the recent renewal. He kept looking at the picture, then at me, not sure we were the same. Then he ordered me out of my car and ushered me into a small room where I was told to wait. I peeked outside and could see that my car was being thoroughly searched with mirrors and wands.

I was cross-examined. Why was I traveling alone? Where was my luggage? How many times had I been arrested? When did I last get out of prison? I explained about the boat, but that only aroused more suspicion. One of the agents finally remembered reading about the accident in the paper. "Please call the American consulate. They'll verify my story," I pleaded.

I started to sweat, and my active imagination placed me in a mystery novel about a tourist who disappears and surfaces years later after having been forced to spy for a foreign country. Three hours later, I was released. Shaken, I arrived at the boatyard, but everyone was too busy with the crisis of the fallen prop to pay attention to my drama.

And meanwhile the sky was falling—Skylab the space station, that is. Rumors had it that it would fall on Bonn, Germany, and a nuclear winter would follow.

After the boat was settled into its new home, it was time for Victor to return to his practice in Los Angeles. The parts for repairing the boat had to be sent from the United States, and he was told it could take up to six weeks. David and I agreed to remain behind to oversee the repairs—and wait for Skylab. The space station debris fell into the Indian Ocean near Australia instead, without disturbing the weather. I took that as a good omen.

While waiting for parts and repair, we had many adventures, but thankfully, none of them involved accidents or law enforcement officers. We met a panoply of characters and shared meals with them, visited their homes, and heard their life stories. Using our Citroen, we traveled through Germany,

Switzerland, Austria, France, Belgium, and the Netherlands, visiting many of their treasured sites.

When Victor returned two months later, the boat was ready for its next adventure.

CHAPTER 12

Letting Go in India

YOUNG ENOUGH TO BE brave and old enough to know better,
I agreed to go with Whizzy to India. When I announced
the plan to my roommates, they cried out in unison, "Are
you crazy?" I knew how difficult Whizzy could be, but I was
desperate enough to get away, so I ignored their words. The
nagging headache that followed my decision foretold what was
to unfold. Most everyone I knew who traveled to India went
because they were on a spiritual journey, but I went to heal
from a broken heart. Perhaps the two are pretty much the same.

In the 1970s, I lived in Sunset Beach in a large drafty
house on the sand in Southern California. My bedroom on
the third floor, a converted attic, became my haven. At night
I heard the roar of breaking waves and smelled the pungent
odor of sea life. Five of us rented the house: Cora, Denise,
Mattie, Whizzy, and I. On that beach I met Michael, or
whatever his name was; one friend called him Rich, others
called him Andy, and he introduced himself to me as Michael.

Later I learned the reason for the confusion when I sneaked a look into a drawer in his apartment and discovered four passports. What was he doing with so many? Earlier, he had told me that he was a professional gambler. He even revealed how he was arrested in South Africa after being accused of cheating in a card game in which he'd won a lot of money; he was eventually released because nobody could prove he had cheated. But I thought his stories were a cover for his real job, that of being a spy. He never stayed long in one place, and he was always off to some exotic country. One moon-bathed warm night he gave me a ring that he said he had won in a poker game and after a kiss said, "Wait for me." Then he disappeared. For months I mourned him in my attic room, and like a sea captain's wife, I stood beside the small window and daily scanned the beach, waiting for his reappearance. When I believed he wasn't coming back, I decided to run away to India with Whizzy.

I charged most of the trip to my credit card, planning to spend the next several years of my life paying it off. Whizzy was the only one of us who never had financial worries. Her father was her banker and even paid for her annual visits to India, while the rest of our parents were merely trying to survive. Whizzy left for India several weeks before me with plans to stay at an ashram and master the art of meditation. We were all hopeful that the lessons would take and make her more humble. I could spare only ten days (counting weekends) away from work, so the plan was that I would meet her in Delhi on the day of the Hindu Diwali celebration, a holy day symbolizing the victory of light over darkness. I thought it fitting: perhaps in India I would find a light that would lighten my dark state of mind. My plane descended amid showers of red, blue, gold, and white-hot fireworks.

The first sign validating my worry about traveling with Whizzy came when her driver met me at the airport. He explained that she had phoned him from the ashram and would not arrive until the next day. Truthfully, I was relieved. The long flight in a cramped coach seat left me ready for bed. By the time we arrived at the hotel, the driver and I were well acquainted. Before we parted in the lobby, he inquired in a manner of earnest curiosity, "Are you truly a friend of Miss Whizzy?" I nodded. He shook his head in disbelief, but I was too tired to explore his reaction.

Sometime around noon the next day, I was wakened by a soft rap on the door. I opened it to find an Indian man in a hotel uniform. "Please, miss. Could you come? We have a problem with your friend, Miss Whizzy," he pleaded.

I dressed quickly, not asking the problem, and upon entering the lobby witnessed a whirlwind of a scene. The reception clerk pleaded with Whizzy, waving his arms in exasperation. "But it is our best room," he kept repeating. Whizzy, dressed in a flowing caftan with large jeweled rings on every finger and a bindi, a red dot, on her forehead, shouted back, "I don't believe you."

"For goodness' sake, Whizzy, what is the problem?" I asked anxiously.

Simply, she wanted a nicer room. "Let's go look at it," I suggested. Upon seeing her spacious room with a great view and decorated with a canopied bed, I grabbed her arm and steered her to my room, which was a bit larger than a closet with a bed the size of a cot.

Too tired to be kind, I snapped, "Get a grip and try using your new learned meditation. You are a guest in this country, not a princess." She pursed her lips into a tight curve, shrugged, and then walked back to her well-appointed room.

That was the beginning of her constant demands for special treatment. From then on, at each hotel, she insisted on the best room, often demanding changes. I began to dread meals, which always began with elaborate instructions on how she wanted her food prepared. She insisted we hire a private driver rather than joining the group we had signed up with. She pouted and threw childlike tantrums whenever I socialized with the others at cocktail hour. Although we had paid to travel with them, Whizzy informed me that we didn't need to associate with "those people," with the implication that they didn't meet her standards. One of "those people" was a concert pianist and two of the couples owned an exclusive hunting resort along Lake Michigan, but that didn't matter to her. There's no other word for it, she was a *nightmare* of a travel companion.

My headache worsened. How could I escape without severing our relationship? Before I could formulate a plan, nature intervened. I became ill. Grateful that I'd seen the Taj Mahal, I didn't care if I missed the rest of our tour. We were staying outside of Udaipur in a compound belonging to a descendant of the former maharajah of the region. My room overlooked gardens of scarlet and salmon-colored bougainvillea and colorful scented blossoms of an array of exotic plants; peacocks roamed freely and called incessantly for a mate, insensitive to my need for quiet as I lay dying.

Whizzy burst into my room and asked, "Why aren't you packed? Our driver is waiting."

"I'm too sick to travel. I'll stay here until I'm better; I'll meet up with you in Pushkar." That was the group's destination after a two-night stay in Jodhpur.

"You can't stay here. You've got to get up," she demanded.

I just pulled the covers over my head and moaned. It wasn't until I made a mad dash for the bathroom to vomit that she left in disgust. I was relieved that she didn't have enough compassion to stay.

My fever raged through the day. The maharajah's heir himself, the owner, came to check on me. After feeling my forehead, he sent for his physician, who gave me an ancient Ayurvedic herbal remedy, and by evening I felt better. I spent three days in the generous care of Indian hospitality, where good food and genuine concern nursed me back to health. After the third day, his "highness," as I affectionately called him, offered his personal driver, Akram, to escort me to Pushkar to meet up with my group—and Whizzy.

I sat like a princess in the back of a Mercedes limousine but insisted the glass partition remain open so I could talk with Akram. A nonstop drive through the Rajasthan desert should have gotten us to Pushkar in five hours, but we didn't drive nonstop. Some distance into the desert, we came upon a temple rising like a jewel on a barren mound.

"What is that?" I asked, pointing to the structure.

"It is a temple to Vishnu. It's beautiful. Would you like to see it?" Akram asked.

We climbed the many steep steps to the top and entered a small terracotta temple with crenelated arches and cool tiled floors. It was a sanctuary from the heat outside. We walked in silence through the rooms and stood quietly looking across the wide, empty land below. *Who comes here*, I wondered, *for such beauty so far from anywhere?*

Akram must have read my thoughts. "It is here for people like us, those who need to stop rushing and thank Vishnu for this day."

"Tell me about Vishnu," I asked.

"He is the god of protection, also the restorer of Karma. Vishnu has hundreds of names, each describing a quality or attribute."

My eyes rested on the beautiful carvings of this god. A statue of him with four arms was draped with garlands of fresh flowers. I looked around for a priest or visitor who might have brought them, but no other people were present.

We drove on until Akram suggested we stop for something to eat. We pulled into an out-of-the-way mini mall with a cafe and a few shops. The outside heat hit me as if I were entering an oven. I couldn't tell if my fever was returning or if it was the oppressive heat that created an urgency to get out of my clothes. I wandered into one of the shops, where a single woman sat sewing. I fingered the colorful, delicate fabrics and I wanted to buy something. The woman understood and, without the aid of English, she selected an outfit for me. I walked out fitted in a kurta tunic top with loose harem pants made of fabric so light it felt like air on my skin. In desperation for relief from the heat, I had spent the entire amount I had brought on the trip for souvenirs.

Akram smiled when he saw my new outfit. "Nice. You are growing into India."

After we dined, we drove on toward Pushkar. We arrived at the tented city where two hundred thousand locals and tourists mingled in the twilight. A cacophony of voices and sounds, a kaleidoscope of colorful saris and tunics, and the overpowering odor of urine, camel, leather, and spices flooded my senses. Akram found the check-in area for American tourists where the tour guide awaited our arrival. I was assigned a small cabana-like structure; it was furnished with only a cot and chair but thankfully had a private area for the toilet and shower. Most tourists resided in tent structures. International tourists' accommodations were arranged in areas according to their nationalities. Even our dining location was assigned by the language we spoke. The purpose, I suppose, was to prevent a Tower of Babel calamity since foreigners came from countries around the world. I learned Whizzy was located a few buildings away from me, and I asked that she not be told of my arrival until morning. I still felt weak from the respiratory ailment and the heat. I wasn't up to a stormy greeting. I skipped dinner and went to bed.

I woke at first light, around five o'clock, eager to explore my surroundings. I found myself on a road of numerous hotels that bordered the holy Pushkar Lake. Crowds gathered on the steep ghats descending to the water's edge; many people had begun bathing in the waters. Desiring a closer look, I made my way inside one of the hotels, hoping to find an area for viewing. I took the elevator to the top floor and searched for a door that might lead to the roof. I passed a room with a door ajar and peered inside. In the center, a large round table was laden with pastries, juices, and covered dishes of food. Across the room I spotted a sizable balcony overlooking the lake below. Thinking this must be a public area, I walked in and headed straight to the balcony. I stood transfixed at the scene below as I watched the colorful crowds chanting as they dipped and rose in the morning's sparkling water.

A voice asked, "Are you having breakfast with us?"

Startled, I turned to find a brown-skinned man with a towel draped around his waist and droplets of water from his recent shower reflecting colors onto his thick, dark hair.

I could hardly find my words. "I'm sorry. I thought—"

Before I could finish, he laughed and said, "Please stay. I'll dress and we'll watch the bathers together. Help yourself." He pointed toward the table. Then he disappeared.

When he returned, we watched in silence as the bathers wandered farther into the lake to make room for the throngs behind them waiting their turn. The morning light that earlier made the lake sparkle now revealed brown and muddy water. Naïve and unworldly, I asked, "Don't they have a place to shower?"

He didn't laugh. He patiently explained how this was a pilgrimage for many. They came to wash in the holy lake in faith, to be cleansed of their sins, some hoping it would cure them of an infirmity.

I replied, "There is a Bible story about that in the Old Testament. It's about a leper who sought relief from his disease. He was told by the prophet to go bathe in the Jordan River seven times. The leper didn't believe the prophet and argued with him, but eventually he went and did what he was told. And he was healed."

"I see. There may be something in these waters that heals also," he responded.

"It looks more like it could give a disease," I muttered.

"Yes, through your eyes I can see that."

During our conversation, I learned that his name was Roshan and that he was traveling with the minister of tourism for India. They came to film the Pushkar Fair, one of India's biggest tourist attractions. He told me that the fair was held during the time of Purnima, the full moon in October or November, and was a place for tribal gathering where villagers from all around came to buy and sell camels and to trade and sell their art. Over time it became attractive to tourists as well, who eventually came in swarms to enjoy the camel races, to camp out and celebrate with the locals, and, of course, to spend money.

"So what do you think of India?" he asked.

I have three types of comebacks when I answer a stranger's question. Sometimes I try to be witty, but that works only about 10 percent of the time because I'm not that clever, and it usually stops the conversation. Or I try to show off my knowledge; that works about 30 percent of the time, and the conversation drags because it's boring. With Roshan, I could do neither. His large, serious eyes took me to a place I reserve for when I feel it's safe to be vulnerable. Deep inside myself I struggled to give him an honest answer.

"I can't get it. It can feel so chaotic, and then I see two women walking down a dirt path in beautiful colored saris and it changes to something peaceful. There is a pink glow to the light that bathes the land, and I'm told that it's the dirt particles in the air that give it its beauty. And then there's the scent of spice mixed with the stink of cow dung and urine. India caused me to be sick, but that came like a gift, rescuing me from an unpleasant situation. It's so confusing. So overwhelming."

"Yes, India is full of contradictions." He smiled.

We were joined by several of his crew members, who began helping themselves to the layout of food. The conversation became lively with plans for their day, and then surprisingly, Roshan asked if I had plans and if I would like to hang out with them. I could hardly suppress my happiness. It was as if the mysticism that permeated the country had a hand in guiding me toward some mysterious destiny.

Most of the day, we followed the crew as they interviewed tourists from around the world. I learned there were five hundred temples, big and small, in the vicinity. Roshan and I visited the largest and most prominent Brahma temple. We viewed the shaved and painted camels, we watched the camels race, and we walked among the stalls filled with souvenirs.

"You are not like most Americans. You're not shopping."

I laughed. "It's because I spent all my money on an Indian outfit so that I could get some relief from the heat."

"Will you wear it this evening?" Then he stopped. "I'm sorry. That's not a way to invite someone to dinner. Will you join us at the hotel? Everyone will be wrapping up and it's a grand finale before we depart tomorrow."

"Yes, I'd love to. I leave tomorrow also, and we head back to Delhi, where we will spend a few days. Then I fly home."

By this time, I felt that Roshan was a true friend. He had a way of shining light into the deepest parts of my soul. I told him about Michael and Whizzy, and here's what he told me.

Referring to Whizzy, he said, "A person carries a heavy burden when there's a need to be special."

And about Michael, he said, "You'll have to decide whether to make his life choices yours, or to define and follow your own."

But then he added something that caught me off guard: "When you've healed yourself, you will stop collecting broken people."

"What do you mean?"

He paused and carefully chose his words. "It's a form of letting go: to stop feeling responsible for someone else's choices, to stop allowing another's personal storm to undermine you, to stop filling up your life with others' dramas."

I caught my breath. *Did he see those things in me?* I wondered. But he wasn't finished. He continued.

"Here—in India, at least—one must find an inner place of stillness or they could become lost in the turbulence of life around them."

It would take years before I fully understood his words of wisdom.

That evening, I arrived at the hotel where the ministry of tourism for India group was holding its farewell dinner. My newly purchased clothes brought applause from the crew. While I was standing on the balcony, with the holy lake filled with bathers behind me, a microphone suddenly appeared, and a glaring light beamed into my face. The cameraman pointed the large black eye of his camera straight at me. I thought the crew members were doing a pantomime of the day. I gave impersonal answers to their questions about what brought me to India and to the Pushkar Fair. Then I was asked, "Tell us, what you think of India?" Then I realized that they were filming.

It was the same question that had started my day. I thought for a moment and then looked past the camera into Roshan's large brown eyes and they steadied me. I answered, "At first, India felt like a violent tidal wave about to knock me off my feet. And I felt lost and overwhelmed. I couldn't get it into focus, all its contradictions. Then, after coming here to Pushkar, I found that when I let go and let the force of it carry me, I began to feel a part of it. It's like I found something here that I can keep."

The interviewer asked, "And what was that?"

I hesitated, then told the world what I'd learned. "How to stay steady amidst chaos and uncertainty. That's all."

Roshan spoke. "That's a wrap. Get it to the studio for the ten o'clock. news program."

And that's how I happened to appear on India's evening news. I think our tour guide was the only one of our group to see it, for he thanked me for my words. The next day, after sadly saying goodbye to Roshan and the others and thanking them for making Pushkar such a memorable experience, I rode with Whizzy back to Delhi. She confessed how she missed me, and I caught her up on the days we'd been separated, but I didn't tell her about my day with Roshan. Sometimes a treasure found is best held close to the heart. I didn't want to jeopardize it by exposing it to possible censure. Indeed, it was never shared—until now.

Whizzy remained the same, but I saw her with new eyes. She had alienated everyone around her, and she looked so lonely, so unfriended, that I could not turn away from her. She would always be who she was, even with the help of meditation; there would always be a storm swirling around her, a storm she created, but it was her storm, not mine. We found a balance during our last days in Delhi and enjoyed the sites and the city together.

The darkness engulfing me when I arrived in India had disappeared. I knew that when—if—I saw Michael, Andy, Rich, or whoever he was, he could not break my heart. Whether he was a gambler, a spy, or just a wanderer, that was not the life for me. In India I learned to stay steady in the midst of uncertainty and to trust being guided by my own light.

CHAPTER 13

Farewell, Neverland

by Dr. David Wardell

As I revealed in the preface to this collection of stories, I went through a time of organizing and shredding, and I came across a story written by my beloved deceased husband. I could have rewritten it in my words, ramping up the drama, because I lived through this with him. Believe me, he understated the drama. He didn't mention the moonless night, crouching in the dark to avoid being detected, and the panic when the bolt cutters failed us and we had to return for another tool. Nor could he know of the gripping panic I felt when I learned he was missing. But it is his story, told in his voice. And it pleases me to share it with you.

SAYING GOODBYE TO A boat is like breaking off an ambivalent love affair: heartbreak and relief. Our relationship with *Neverland* began when we stole her. I suppose there are some things one shouldn't tell about oneself, but indeed, I was a two-time boat thief, and the second time, I nearly didn't make it.

The first time, my wife and I dressed in black, darkened our faces, and waited for midnight. We slipped under the fence of the boatyard, cut the padlock on our newly purchased boat, and pushed the boat out of its slip into the harbor, where we then motored to a secured slip. This was done at our attorney's suggestion—the only way we might resolve the dispute with the dealer to replace the defective stanchions that came with our new boat. It worked. Without the boat, the dealer agreed to a lower price if we replaced the stanchions ourselves. We then took rightful possession of our beautiful Hans Christian thirty-six-foot cutter. We christened her *Neverland*.

The saying is true that the two happiest days in a boater's life are the first day he owns his boat and the day he sells it. After many years of adventures, we sold *Neverland*.

Within months of the purchase, the buyer found himself in a divorce. For two years we'd been sympathetic and patient with the sporadic payments and his difficulties; finally, however, the payments ceased altogether with his declaring that he could not afford any more payments. Yet he refused to return the boat.

Herein was the problem. Although we had a contractual security interest in the boat, we had a second security interest in the buyer's home in Oregon. But you see, the boat was anchored in the state of Washington. In checking with lawyers, we were informed one cannot legally repossess the boat in Washington State unless the house is foreclosed on first. Yet in Oregon, one is required to foreclose on the boat before taking action against the house. Only one solution was offered: while I could not seek possession of the boat through the courts in

Washington State, it was perfectly legal for me to personally retake possession of the boat!

When I told my wife that I planned to "steal" *Neverland* again, she yawned and said, "Been there, done that," but obligingly dropped me off at the airport. *Neverland* was berthed at Bainbridge Island, a stone's throw from Seattle.

I departed on a beautiful warm, sunny Southern California day with an eager prospective buyer. On arriving at lovely Eagle Harbor, we were met by a pretty college student who was renting the boat and living aboard. I explained the problem and she was surprisingly cooperative; she agreed to move in with her grandmother if we helped pack her belongings. The move took most of the day. The buyer left in our rental car after we agreed to meet at a marina farther down the coast. I finally left the slip at dusk.

The first thing I discovered on leaving was that the fuel gauge read empty. I knew I could make it to the nearest fuel dock, but when I got there it was closed. The wind began to pick up, threatening a storm, so I decided to sail to the harbor a few miles down the coast, hoping to make it there before the weather turned too severe.

Rapidly, the storm increased in intensity and it was difficult to sail single-handed. The snow turned to sleet, and the winds grew stronger. There was no foul-weather gear aboard and all I'd brought with me was a light Members Only jacket. Soon I was shivering so violently that I could hardly steer the boat. I looked around for a place to dock, but the dark came fast and the falling snow obscured my vision. I began to panic, thinking I'd have to abandon the boat if necessary and swim to shore.

Just about that time I came upon a blazing light; as I approached it a posted sign read, "Danger, Do Not Enter, Property of US Navy." In the distance I could barely make out a naval vessel, some sort of tug with no signs of life, so I headed straight for it. As I came alongside her, I cast a line aboard. A sailor appeared on deck and helped secure the line to the stanchion on the tug. He could see that I was shaking from the cold. He took me to the skipper, where I pled my case. They offered me a bowl of hot soup and a berth for the night, promising to provide all the fuel I'd need in the morning so that I could continue my journey.

Meanwhile, back in Southern California, it was one o'clock in the morning when the telephone at my house rang. It was the wife of the prospective buyer calling my wife.

"Have you heard from your husband?" she asked.

"Not since around five o'clock tonight. He was just heading out."

"He didn't arrive at the agreed-upon place to meet my husband. Give him a message when you hear from him that my husband has checked into the Best Western and will wait for him." My stunned wife was about to hang up when the woman added, "By the way, a huge storm has moved into the area. It's snowing."

Now what does a woman do when her husband goes missing in a snowstorm at sea? She wakes her best friend to come sit with her. They began calling the airport to make reservations to leave on the first morning flight, and also, I am told, cleaned out the refrigerator. "Well, I had to feel like I was doing something constructive, to do something to calm my nerves," my wife later explained.

Finally, she came upon another solution. Her brother was a lieutenant commander with the Coast Guard. So, she awakened him in Washington, DC, at five thirty his time. He immediately puts out an all-points bulletin.

My brother-in-law has influence. This I know because once when my wife and I were sailing in the Channel Islands I was awakened out of sleep by a bullhorn calling, "Ahoy, *Neverland*, prepare for boarding."

After stumbling out of bed, I climbed to the deck and was greeted by three uniformed Coast Guard men in a dinghy, one with a semiautomatic gun pointed at our boat. Two men boarded us, ostensibly "to check safety equipment." But I became suspicious as they searched under floorboards and in the bilge. When my wife had had just about enough, she said to the sailor closest to her, "My brother is in the Coast Guard."

"Oh yeah? What's his name?"

When she gave his name, he laughed out loud and said, "Small world! He defended me in my trial. He got me off too. A damn fine attorney."

"What was your case?" she asked.

"Drugs," he mumbled.

He then gave a loud whistle to his buddy and said, "It's okay. Let's go." He winked at her and said as he was climbing into the dinghy, "Say hi to your brother."

My brother-in-law upheld his reputation this time too. I was awakened by the skipper of the Navy vessel about three in the morning. "Are you Dr. Wardell?" he asked. I nodded. "You have friends in high places. There's an all-points search for you ordered from headquarters. We've got a message for you: you're to call home."

And I did.

After a hearty breakfast, five gallons of fuel, and better weather conditions, I took off and met the new buyer at the agreed-upon anchorage. The rest of the transaction was uneventful: under regulations, the boat was put up for sale, the previous buyer appeared but did not make an offer, and the new buyer bought the boat, paying off our interest in it in full.

PART III

Reflections

The best part of human language,
properly so called,
is derived from reflection
on the acts of the mind itself.

—SAMUEL TAYLOR COLERIDGE, *BIOGRAPHIA LITERARIA*

CHAPTER 14

Beliefs

I HAVE OFTEN WONDERED about the randomness of life. How is it that one person escapes danger and another succumbs? A friend who grew up in South Africa told me that before he joined the British Army in World War II, the local witch doctor "threw the bones" and foretold that he would travel over a great water and that one day he would safely return. Several times during the war a bullet grazed him, only to find another victim close by. Does what we believe predict our outcome? Does a positive thought act as a protective shield? Perhaps not always. But I can tell you a story of when a belief definitely saved my life.

As a young and idealistic college student, I felt it was my duty to make the world a better place. I planned to fulfill this dream by becoming a bush pilot in South America, flying medical supplies to small villages. I'd been romantically influenced by having just read Beryl Markham's *West with the Night*, the autobiography of the first female pilot to cross the

Atlantic nonstop. Also, I was dating an airline pilot as idealistic as I. His ambition was to save the planet from environmental pollution. There we were—two dreamers.

He was an exacting flight teacher, willing to nudge me toward my goal, and I was an eager student. In my first lesson, I spent several hours above the Salton Sea, a partially dried-up lakebed, learning to "land on a dime." After a few hours of touch-and-gos, I began to get the hang of "picking a spot"— that is, setting a landing pattern, trimming to the perfect glide ratio, and then slipping the plane down so the wheels touched at the designated spot.

"You've got her. Take us in," my instructor said as we approached home base. I proudly made my first official landing at a commercial airport—after only one lesson! Filled with joy, I hopped out of the plane and blew a kiss to the sky.

My instructor, Cowboy, loved flying of any kind; barn-storming, pylon racing, dogfighting with his buddies. He earned the nickname "Cowboy" because of his daring style— for example, he did a loop during his descent while coming in for a landing. Together, Cowboy and *Angel*, his plane, were fearless and competent. He took risks to learn the stuff his plane was made of. Flying close to commercial jets, he'd demonstrate the danger of jet wash and downdraft. "It's killed some of the best," he told me, referring to other pilots as we were buffeted wildly. Another time, he cut the engine on takeoff to scare into me the reflex of restarting the engine and at all times scanning the control panel for possible problems. Once when flying calmly to a picnic site at an out-of-the-way airport, he suddenly rolled the plane. He explained, "Banning Pass, outside Palm Springs, is famous for its wind funnels; it can flip a plane upside down without warning. We'll do it again, and you take the controls and right her." We flew in fog, where he taught me to fly straight and level by reading the instruments. *Angel*, the tail-dragger biplane, braved Santa Ana winds—facing headwinds so fierce the plane actually flew backward. We did spins and rolls; we teased clouds with lazy eights (a 180-degree turn with a climb) and chandelle maneuvers (somewhat like an S-turn across a road but with a climb and descent). Cowboy explained that one must master these before getting licensed because they teach the pilot about control precision under a variety of conditions.

He must have thought I'd mastered them because after only fourteen hours of instruction, he announced after a flight, "You're ready. Tomorrow you go on your first cross-country flight, solo."

Cross-country meant filing a flight plan, picking a destination at least one hundred miles away, and calculating the best navigation route.

Solo! Alone? My heart raced and my breath grew shallow. I mean, it's one thing to fly backward and upside down, chase clouds, and race winds, when you have Cowboy in the copilot seat. But what if something truly went wrong? Would I remember everything I'd learned?

I choked out the words, "Don't most students fly solo after twenty hours or more?"

"Some do. Some don't. You're ready."

Reading my face with the same instinct with which he read his plane, he said firmly, "You never have to die in a small plane. Even when you can't find a place to sit down. If you're headed into a mountain, just drop your flaps, slow 'er down, and close to the ground pull up the nose and make her stall; the plane will drop instead of flying forward. Bail out just before you hit."

Easy for him to say.

"I've had to land *Angel* on a barge out on the ocean when she wouldn't start up after flying her upside down."

Still sensing my fear that something could go wrong, he held my face in his hands and made me look him in the eyes, *"You must believe what I said about not dying in a small plane. Tell me you believe!"* I nodded.

The next day I headed for Palm Springs to log my first long-distance solo cross-country. The day was sweltering, so hot that the runway shimmered as if an oasis lay ahead. I'd rented a two-seater Cessna 150 from a flight school at the airport. The plane felt sluggish in the heat and took more runway than usual to lift off. But once aloft, it dipped and rose happily as it caught a thermal. I broke into song, as excited as when I got a driver's license. This was a new sort of independence.

Less than thirty minutes out, the tachometer began to fluctuate. I'd heard about vapor locks and thought, *Oh, not here, not over these mountains,* and I began to search for my spot. I saw a good one, a long stretch of road between two mountains. But then the engine picked up and purred steadily, and I breathed a sigh of relief. I increased my altitude, hoping the air was cooler higher up in case it was the heat that had threatened a vapor lock. I heard another little sputter, and the engine went back to normal. Two more, then all was well again. But I was starting to get nervous because I could see ahead of me the steep, jagged peaks of the San Jacinto Mountains, which I had to cross.

What should I do? Turn back? Undecided, I put out a pan-pan call; that tells whoever is listening that there's a pilot in trouble, but it's not a Mayday crisis. Mayday means you're going down! March Air Force Base personnel picked up my call and I explained the problem. Using an automatic direction finder to try to locate me on radar, they ordered me to fly at a selected heading for thirty seconds and then turn to another heading for another thirty seconds. I realized that this was going to throw off all my careful calculations of my course to Palm Springs, but I complied. They couldn't find me, so they kept directing me to fly at various headings, one of which took me straight toward a peak of the San Jacinto Mountains; I veered sharply away from it. They thought I was close to the Mexican border, but I said I didn't think so. But who knew? I had lost track of time and space and was hovering somewhere on the edge of infinity. Then we lost radio contact. Frantic, I got busy reading my map, looking for my spot, and trying to calculate a heading that would take me to Palm Springs—all at the same time.

Then it happened: one big sputter and the engine stopped. *This is it!* Now where is that spot? It's way behind me. All I could see below were jagged peaks. I radioed a Mayday. My throat was dry, and my armpits were wet. A controller from Imperial Valley Airport responded in a calm voice. I grasped at it as if it would save me, but the communication broke up with static. I told him, "I'm going down" and I heard his crackling words over the headphones, "Watch out for the power lines."

What power lines? If only I could see some since they're usually located next to a road, and a road is as good as a runway.

So, this is how it ends? For a moment, all I could see was the disappointed look on Cowboy's face. A violent thermal snapped me back to the emergency and I heard his voice: "You never have to die in a small plane." *This is not how I'm going out,* shouted an inner voice.

Then I saw below me a snakelike thin silver line, not long, but long enough for a short field landing. I set up a descent pattern gliding toward my "spot." *Oh, no, a truck wants the same space. Drop more flaps, slow 'er down. Now turn downwind, now turn on final. Runway straight ahead.* And then as though it were a regular, everyday landing, I flew over the truck and landed behind it going the opposite direction—a perfect touchdown on the winding, narrow road. The truck kept going, unaware or unconcerned about the drama that had just unfolded.

Ecstatic to be on terra firma, I radioed a flippant report. "The *Eagle* has landed," I informed the world. Only static responded. I climbed out of the plane, pushed it off the road, and waited to be rescued. An hour passed with no sign of traffic. Hot and thirsty, I thought I could make it to a small house I'd seen from the air. But after attempting to walk in flip-flops on a sweltering tarred road, I quickly abandoned the plan. *Maybe it was safer to stay with the plane anyway,* I reasoned.

Finally, I spotted a car! I leaped up from where I'd been sitting in the shade of the wing and waved frantically. The travelers stared in disbelief at the petite female in a hot pink miniskirt and a halter top jumping up and down next to a misplaced airplane. They must have determined this was a setup—maybe drug dealers. They accelerated as they passed.

Hours went by as I waited. I began to envision a night of hiding from jackals in a cramped cockpit. Close to sundown I saw a plane circling overhead. After five flybys the pilot touched down in a small twin engine plane and rolled a few yards past me, his wing just missing my plane. He opened the door and shouted over the roar of the engine, "Good god, girl, how did you ever get in here?" Later he confessed, "I've got over twenty thousand hours and nearly didn't make it. How many do you have?"

He'd been flying a commercial airliner from John Wayne Airport in Orange County to Imperial Valley Airport and heard my Mayday call as he was passing overhead. He saw me circling below him and witnessed my safe landing. After landing at Imperial Valley Airport, his home base, he went up to the tower to inquire about me. "I heard the female pilot's Mayday call on our radio. Has a search-and-rescue team been sent out? Anyone picked her up yet?"

"Not yet. We think she killed herself. She sounded pretty scared."

"I saw her land. I know exactly where. I'll take my plane and go pick her up."

I flew back to the airport with the pilot in his plane, leaving mine parked by the side of the road. He invited me to have dinner with his family, and they put me up for the night. The next day we drove back to my Cessna with a mechanic and a supply of fuel. It turned out that the flying school where I had rented the plane had gotten a batch of contaminated fuel. Later I was told that two other planes rented from the same flying school had crashed, including one carrying a family. There had been no survivors.

The mechanic cleaned the carburetor and refueled the plane. Although I was nervous about getting back in the cockpit, I knew it had to be done. I wanted to go home. After saying goodbye to my rescuer and thanking him for his heroic deed, it was time to face my fear. The mechanic walked down the road to stop any oncoming traffic. I flew the plane off the road and back to home base. As I entered the airport's airspace and requested permission to land, the controller said, "Welcome home, pilot." The applause from the other controllers brought a proud smile to my face. As I came down the glide slope I broke into song: "Sweet Caroline," good times never felt so good.

I continued to fly despite the engine failure scare and eventually qualified for a commercial ticket. That means that I could take off in poor visibility because I knew how to fly by my instruments. I didn't want to take any chances in the sky.

I asked Cowboy what he had thought when he learned that the plane hadn't made it to Palm Springs. You see, when one files a flight plan and the plane doesn't arrive at the airport, a dispatch is sent out notifying the departing airport. So the tower had notified the flight school where I had rented the plane. Cowboy was at the school when the notification came in.

"I wasn't worried. I knew you could land on a dime," he said, smiling confidently.

It's a great feeling to have someone believe in you. But in this case, it was more important that I believed him. It saved me—I'm certain of it.

CHAPTER 15

The Green Book

FOR MANY YEARS I owned a house on a small island in British Columbia. The population consisted of four hundred permanent residents, which swelled to nearly twelve hundred in the summer months. I spent my summers there kayaking, writing, and getting to know the islanders.

My remote Canadian island had a wireless, high-speed underground network without any of the advantages of modern technology. The old-fashioned name for it is word of mouth. Before the RCMP (Royal Canadian Mounted Police) Mountie could tie his boat to the ferry dock, islanders knew to keep unregistered vehicles off the road, wear seat belts when driving, and come to a full stop at the only stop sign on the island. Otherwise, islanders were routinely casual about these things.

Before being connected to this network, I had the misfortune of being stopped by our sole visiting officer. My license plate revealed that the insurance on my red ragtop GM Tracker had lapsed. Also, I had driven the one-half mile to the "upper store" without my driver's license in my possession. The officer followed me back to the house so he could verify that I had a valid license. When I explained that I had just arrived on the island and had not yet been in town to register the car, he was sympathetic. We had barely stepped into the house when the phone rang—and not just once. He smiled when each time I whispered to the caller, "Call me later. I'll tell you about it when he leaves." He left on friendly terms and without giving me a citation.

On our island, there was also a hotline run by Florence Waddington. She lived at the end of the island, in full view of the lighthouse, and kept vigilant watch for the comings and goings of the orcas. One Sunday morning my phone rang, and Flo's excited voice gave a report on the orcas: "They came around the point about three this morning and, if they keep to their schedule, should be back at the rocks by noon." I glanced at the clock: eleven-thirty. I jumped into the Tracker, where I always kept a folding chair, a blanket, and a book, and I raced to the sculptured rocks.

The rocks are located near the lighthouse at the end of the island where the tides meet. It is a favorite feeding site for the orcas. The rocks are roughly shaped in the form of animals: a whale, a fish, an eagle, and a turtle. Some say that they were shaped by natural erosion caused by the sea and wind; others say they that they were carved by the Indians who over the centuries inhabited the island.

Arriving at the rocks, I placed my chair on the back of the turtle rock and sat down to wait for the orcas. Within half an hour I heard the swooshing sound of orca breath. Two large whales headed toward the rocks—and me. The water appeared to darken as three pods, over one hundred orcas, arrived at their feeding ground. I had been told that orcas love an audience, so I ran along the long back of the whale rock, the rock closest to the water, waving and calling out to them. I tried making musical overtones with my voice. What a show they gave me! Those farther out in the water spy hopped and breached; even the babies surfed and undulated beside their mothers. A huge bull came to scratch his body against the rocks, and we were eye to eye. Suddenly he leaped into the air, and crashed with a belly flop, drenching me. I swear I heard him laugh as he swam on. I looked around to share my glee or surprise with any other visitor, but the rocks were empty. I was the only blessed observer. After the show ended, I fell back onto my chair, exhausted and euphoric.

As I sat there, I spotted something lying on the eagle rock close to the water's edge. A small green book whose cover was embossed with gold letters and a gold filigree wreath bore the title *Rubáiyát of Omar Khayyám*. Puzzled, I noted that it showed no signs of water damage and yet it had rained the night before. Leafing through it, I recalled Omar Khayyám's hedonistic poetry from my college days: "Here with a loaf of bread beneath the bough,/ a flask of wine, a book of verse—and thou/ beside me singing in the wilderness—/ and wilderness is paradise enow." One page revealed that the edition was a careful reprint of the first edition of 1859, and inscribed inside were the words, "Now very rare and not to be found for a half-penny a copy." Folded between the last pages was a yellowed piece of paper—a telegram addressed to a Mrs. Josephine Elizabeth Jones. It informed her that her husband, Robert, had been killed in action during a battle in Italy. It was dated September 21, 1944. I drew a sharp breath. The date was exactly fifty years ago this day.

I looked around expecting—hoping—to find its owner, but the shore was deserted and the forest behind me stood dark and silent. Reading some of the verse—which extolled the beliefs that pleasure is the greatest good, that the glories of this world are better than the paradise that comes after death, and that wine is more trustworthy than philosophers—suited my mood of the moment. But I could not keep the book. It was a treasure that belonged to someone. I needed to find its owner.

When I returned home, I telephoned Mrs. Waddington and asked her if she'd seen anyone at the rocks earlier that morning. "Yes. There was a young woman who stood looking out across the sound. My phone rang, and when I came back with my binoculars to take a look, she was gone."

I pondered this before telephoning Margie Gordimer, the ferry ticket officer, who was known for her photographic memory. She remembered everyone entering and leaving the island by ferry. In fact, her keen memory aided in the capture of two thieves who broke into absent homeowners' houses and departed with a van full of merchandise. "No," she told me when I asked if she'd seen any unfamiliar faces lately, "everyone who came and left the island the last several days were all islanders or family relatives." And she knew them all.

Now my curiosity was piqued. I noted the address on the telegram—a street in James Bay in Victoria. Since I'd be in Victoria shopping the next day, I thought I might drive by and see if the place was still standing.

It was. The houses along the street were modest bungalows with wide porches and groomed yards with rose and rhododendron bushes. I timidly approached the house in question. "Sorry, I've only been here three years," a young woman told me. As I turned to leave, she said, "You might try two doors down. Bertha Forrester has lived here all her life. I think she's in her nineties. She might remember who the prior owners were."

As I walked back to my car, about to give up my search, I saw the curtains move in the house of Mrs. Forrester. I shrugged and thought, *Why not?*

Eager for company Mrs. Forrester invited me in. I told her for whom I was looking, but she wasn't going to put forth any information until I had admired her many pots of African violets and listened to her lengthy life history. She had been a graphologist in her day and had been an expert witness in "some famous trials," she reported. Then she offered to analyze my character if I wrote her a paragraph. According to her analysis, I am an overly sensitive person, wise and generous, but could be crafty and devious dealing in money matters. *What?* That did it—I stopped believing, for I had no sense when it came to money matters. Careful not to offend her and eager to change the subject, I returned to the purpose of my visit.

"Of course, I remember Josephine and Robert. They had just gotten married before they moved here. They honeymooned on one of the Gulf Islands—I can't remember which one. When they returned, they invited everyone on the street to a send-off party for Robert. You see, he was being sent overseas. They were so attractive, so young, and so in love." Mrs. Forrester's face softened and bore such a forlorn expression that one would think she had been the sufferer. "She became a war widow shortly after he went overseas. His death nearly destroyed her."

"Do you know what happened to her?"

"No. She didn't stay around. Went back east, I believe. Had family there. I met her sister, who came here after Robert's death to be with Jo."

Mrs. Forrester could not remember the sister's name. So, our talk drifted to other topics, including my little island. When I mentioned that we had a vineyard on the island, she suddenly brightened and exclaimed. "Now I remember. Champaign."

Seeing my perplexed look, she explained, "The sister. Her name was Irene Champaign. She lived in Saint John, New Brunswick."

I thanked her for the information and the tea, promised I'd visit again, and left with this fragile piece of information. Truly, I was ready to drop the sleuthing and accept the book as a serendipitous treasure. But the mystery of how it came to be on the rocks nagged at me and I couldn't drop the matter.

Giving in to my need for closure, the next day I called the telephone operator and found that there was still a listing in the Saint John directory for an Irene Champaign.

A long silence followed my nervous introduction. Then Irene said, "Jo has been dead for forty-eight years. Two years after Robert's death she went back to the island where she honeymooned. It is believed she threw herself off the rocks into the water, but her body was never found." She confirmed that it happened on my island.

What could I make of this? I don't believe in ghosts. Other dimensions may exist, but I don't believe that one can rip time's veil to sneak a glimpse into the past or future. But what about the book? How did it come to be on the rocks fifty years to the date of the signing of the telegram? If Jo, in her despair, had thrown herself off the rocks and ended her life forty-eight years ago, how did the book appear on the anniversary of her husband's death? Had someone on the island been in possession of it and left it there by accident?

A week later I ran into the RCMP officer at the store and I sat down with him at his table. I felt friendly toward him because he had overlooked my prior violation. Then I told him the story of the green book. He offered to make an inquiry about any missing persons. He reported back to me a few days later: there had been no recent reports of missing persons or floating bodies. But a retired sergeant, a friend of the officer, recalled a story about a young woman by the name of Josephine Elizabeth Jones who had indeed gone missing. The account was that she had been staying at a cottage near the lighthouse. On the day she disappeared, she had been spotted out on the rocks. An orca came by and splashed her with water, like the bull had done with me a few days earlier. The lighthouse keeper said that she apparently slipped into the water while standing too close to the edge. Another witness reported that the woman had been very depressed, and she believed that Josephine threw herself in. Her body was never found.

Well, I suppose some mysteries are never to be revealed.

I learned from Florence Waddington that a legend had risen out of the story and that young lovers were known to visit the site to celebrate their love.

I still have the little book nestled among other books on my bookshelf. How I treasure the carefree words of *Rubáiyát of Omar Khayyám*:

> Oh, come with old Khayyám, and Leave the
> Wise To talk; one thing is certain, that Life flies;
> One thing is certain, and the Rest is Lies;
> The Flower that once has blown for ever dies.

CHAPTER 16

Ghosts and Suitcases

STANDING IN THE KITCHEN of my Canadian island home, barefoot and wet from having just finished showering, I heard a soft knock at the front door. Curiously, I found Agnes Dauphine smiling and extending to me a plate of cookies. More curious, however, was her attire. She wore a to-town dress, which was most uncharacteristic. Perched precariously on her head sat a small pillbox hat with a stiff white feather jutting forward like a pointing finger. What on earth? Islanders didn't dress up and I didn't think any of the women there owned a pair of heels. Seeing that I was not dressed to receive a guest, her warm smile turned quizzical. I racked my brain, trying to piece the puzzle together. Then I remembered a casual meeting and an offhand remark about her dropping by for tea one day. She asked if Sundays were good, and I mumbled something that must have sounded like consent.

She gave me a quick once-over and couldn't hide her disappointment as she examined my wet, ungroomed hair and the rumpled khakis and T-shirt I wore. I invited her in, and the second disappointment came when the tea I poured for her didn't rise to her English standards. I saw her shoulders stiffen, but she valiantly remained polite; she looked away, as though not seeing the tea could alter reality. Finally, she could no longer restrain herself, "You know, we never use tea bags. And of course, what's worse is reusing one," she offered as I refilled my cup by pouring water over the used tea bag. She then revealed having had tea with the cheapest resident on the island, who shamelessly offered her guests tea made with used bags.

I smiled politely and changed the subject and complimented Mrs. Dauphine on the cookies that she had brought. Knowing that I was a newcomer to the island and seeming eager to make a friend, she began a litany of confessions.

Confession number one: "People on the island don't like me," she confidently volunteered.

"Oh?" I said, hardly knowing how to respond.

"You'll hear. They all talk. They call me a gold digger."

"No one's ever said that to me about you," I offered reassuringly.

"It's not like what they think," she hurried on. "I was in real estate when I met my husband. He'd put his house up for sale. Right off, he took a fancy to me. I didn't know he was eighty-nine, and I didn't know he'd die three weeks after we married. He should have told me his age. I'd have not been so"—she searched for the right word—"spirited. You know what I mean?" A pale blush dusted her cheeks.

I nearly choked trying to imagine it. "Well, I'm sure he didn't mind," I said smiling sympathetically.

Confession number two: "I don't socialize with the people around here. I quit going to play bridge. They always deliberately made sure I had the dummy hand."

"Well, I don't know much about bridge, but isn't it the luck of the draw?"

And the confessions continued.

"Even the children call me a witch," she said.

"How cruel," I said indignantly, although I could see the resemblance.

"It started on Halloween night. They came trick-or-treating. I stepped outside on the deck to greet them. I'd been sweeping the kitchen floor and still had the broom in my hand. They saw me with the broom and the whole group backed away and someone started yelling, 'A witch, a witch.' The idea was probably planted in their heads by their parents."

"They were caught up in the spirit of the night, don't you think?" I said, making another attempt to appease her.

"It's all of them. Even old Mr. Kramer who lives on the island a stone's throw from ours, he blames me for his house burning down."

"How could he? You weren't even on his island when it happened. Were you?" I asked, becoming increasingly concerned about her state of mind.

"No, but he knows I can see his place with my binoculars. He's seen me watching. He thinks I should have called the fire department sooner."

"He said that to you?" My voice didn't conceal my disbelief. I'd recently been at a barbeque with the Kramers and they talked about the fire, but Mrs. Dauphine's name never came up.

"Oh, not to me directly, but I know what he thinks."

She changed the subject. "I'd move, but it's my mother. She won't leave."

"I didn't know your mother lived with you." I'd heard that Mrs. Dauphine was a widow and lived alone.

"She does," she said matter-of-factly. She sucked in her breath and let it out slowly. "She's been dead ten years now and she won't leave. When I've talked to her about the problems I'm having here on the island, she says, 'Agnes, I'm not moving again.' I know I should leave, but she won't hear of it. And it's been very hard, very lonely, since my dog died."

"I'm sorry to hear that—about your dog."

I was surprised when she let loose a hearty laugh. "Oh, don't be. You wanna hear something? When he died, I couldn't figure out what to do with him. I didn't want to bury him in my yard because I didn't want another ghost hanging around the place. So, I put him in a suitcase and took it on the ferry to town. Now I wasn't sure where I would leave him, but I figured a spot out near Butchart Gardens would be nice. But I didn't actually have a place in mind."

"Was he a small dog?" I asked, trying to visualize her carrying the suitcase.

"He was a good-sized poodle. So of course, the suitcase was large and heavy. I made it off the ferry all right. You know how you have to take the steps up to the area where you catch the bus? Well, I was struggling up the stairs with this heavy suitcase, and two husky young boys offered to help."

"I told them, 'Your mothers must have done a good job with you lads, teaching you to help out an old woman like me.' They asked where they should leave the suitcase, and I said at the bus stop just outside the exit doors."

"They hurried on ahead. When I arrived at the bus stop there was no suitcase. I asked the bus driver if two boys had dropped off a large suitcase. He said he hadn't seen a suitcase. So, I went looking about for them, thinking they were waiting for me somewhere nearby. But they were nowhere in sight."

She paused and I poured her more hot tea to warm the tea in the cup she had hardly touched.

She leaned forward, and pointing her finger near my face, said with a grin, "The suitcase never appeared. They must have thought I was carrying all my valuable possessions in it. Can you imagine the look on their faces when they opened that suitcase?" She paused holding the teacup in midair, and then said with great satisfaction, "They solved my problem." She took a sip of tea and then put her cup down with such energy that it made me think of the gesture as an exclamation point at the end of a sentence. Then she broke into a laugh bordering on hysteria.

"What did you do?" I asked, imagining her horror at losing her dog to such thieves.

"Well, I turned around and took the next ferry home. What else could I do? My business in town was finished."

I reflected on her answer and nodded in agreement. Suddenly I had an ingenious solution to the problem with her mother. "Why don't you do the same with your mother? Pack her up in a suitcase and drop her off in town. You got rid of one potential ghost, and maybe you could get rid of another. Then she wouldn't be around to interfere with your plans."

The friendly conversation ended abruptly. Mrs. Dauphine stood, brusquely pushed her chair away from the table, and gave me a harsh glare of contempt. The little white feather in her hat quivered as it pointed reproachfully at my face. In a contemptuous and severe tone of voice she informed me, "You are sick." Then without thanking me for the tea, she turned and left the house. And I joined her list of unsuitable, unsociable people.

Mrs. Dauphine's isolation and loneliness pestered my conscience, for I knew that these states contribute to paranoia. Shopping in town the next day, I was still mulling over her dilemma when a way to reconnect with her dawned on me. At a specialty shop selling teas and coffees, I purchased loose leaf Earl Gray tea.

The next afternoon, I appeared on her doorstep wearing a straw sunhat with an enormous sunflower perched on the brim, sandals, and a flowing skirt. She peeked behind the partially opened door and stared suspiciously back at me.

"I've come to ask you to show me how to steep English tea. I apologize for being such an unaware hostess," I said.

A long pause followed, and I feared she'd slam the door shut, but it slowly opened. "Americans are truly ignorant about tea."

"Thank you for understanding," I said with a smile.

With caution, she invited me in. I looked around, wondering where the ghost mother appeared to her. Did she sit at the tidy kitchen table or on the massive couch facing out to the Georgia Straight? Or did she arrive only at bedtime to disturb Mrs. Dauphine's sleep? I noted several curio cabinets filled with romantic porcelain figurines and doilies that decorated antique tabletops—a charming environment.

She served a lovely tea with scones and jam. Indeed, she showed me how to entertain in the English style.

"Did you knit the doilies?" I asked.

And so began our conversation on the topics of her talents, knitting and needlepoint, away from the severity of her mother's threats. I stayed an hour and then excused myself after asking if I could visit again. And so began my weekly drop-ins, which in time became filled with stories of her childhood and the severe and cruel role her domineering mother played. No wonder she hadn't married until after her mother died; she had lived under the thumb of a tyrant, and even after her death, Agnes could not free herself.

During my last visit before returning to the States, she astounded me when she announced that she had decided to move to Victoria. She found a community for seniors that she thought was favorable.

"Is your mother going with you? I asked.

Mrs. Dauphine threw back her head with laughter. "She says she's not moving! And you know what? I didn't give her my new address."

Over time, I reflected on the difference between disposing of a dog in a suitcase and casting aside a ghost mother. I can conclude only that one she was ready to part with and the other she was not. I learned the importance of letting people have their illusions. They surrender them only when they are no longer needed. And in her own way, Agnes Dauphine found a way that suited her to a T(ea).

CHAPTER 17

Six Degrees of Separation

IN 1967, STANLEY MILGRAM, a social psychologist, conducted a study to test the "small-world phenomenon," which inspired the phrase "six degrees of separation." Six degrees of separation is the theory that anyone on earth can be connected to any other person on the planet through a chain of acquaintances with no more than five intermediaries. Milgram decided to test the theory. He wanted to find out how many exchanges it would take to get a letter from a random correspondent in Omaha, Nebraska, to a Boston, Massachusetts, recipient identified only by a brief description. His finding? It took fewer than six steps.

Numerous times while during a casual conversation with a stranger, we have found a common acquaintance. For example, attending a theater performance in Vietnam, I discovered the stranger sitting next to me was from my hometown. Another time, riding an elevator in Hong Kong, I overheard a stranger telling another stranger a story involving a person I knew well.

But the most amazing encounter occurred on an airplane traveling from Los Angeles to Washington, DC.

On the red-eye special, the low-cost midnight flight to DC, the cabin lights dimmed after takeoff and weary passengers gathered up their pillows and blankets to sleep for the five-hour ride. I could not sleep. My mind was filled with anxiety and my heart was full of sorrow.

My brother, whom I had not seen for twelve years, called and asked me to come. The last time I had seen him was when he came to the boarding school I attended during my ninth-grade year. Since he had just finished high school and had no place to go, he came to tell me that he had enlisted in the military. I had not seen him since. The years passed. I learned that he had completed college, and then law school. He had been commissioned as an officer and had risen to the rank of lieutenant commander in the Coast Guard and then went on to become a JAG (judge advocate general). What would he think of his kid sister? Would I measure up? Would he be proud of me? These concerns dominated my mind. But it was the reason for the visit that caused the sorrow.

"Let's visit Naomi," he had said. Stunned, I agreed, but I was puzzled. He had closed the door on our past and never looked back. Then he explained, "I have questions that only she has answers to. Please come, Sis; let's go before it's too late."

Two years earlier, I had sent Naomi a ticket and she had visited me in California. I understood my brother's fear for I had observed Naomi's failing memory. In fact, I'd been so concerned that when I accompanied her to the airplane, I asked the attendant at the check-in counter if someone would keep an eye on her.

Now I sat in the last row on the crowded plane trying to still my mind. My book lay open on my lap, but I could not read. As I looked out the window, I saw nothing but the reflection of my face. My mind drifted to the memories of the only mother I'd known. I remembered the day when it was my turn to leave and I had no place to go, when I went to say goodbye to her. In that painful parting, she released me with love. Now, it was my turn to do the same for her.

I didn't realize that I was crying until I heard a voice ask, "Would you like some water?" I looked up into the face of an attractive stewardess. I nodded. When she returned, she asked if she could sit with me. Perhaps she asked since I was the only passenger still awake, or maybe it was because the seat next to me was the last empty seat at the back of the plane.

"Are you headed home on break?" she asked, glancing at the book on my lap.

I realized that it was Easter week and the plane must have been filled with students. As happens with strangers on airplanes, we began an intimate conversation, perhaps more personal than I intended.

"No. I'm going to visit my brother. I haven't seen him in twelve years."

"Were you close?"

"As young children, yes. But life events landed us on different ends of the continent."

Then she asked a pivotal question, the kind of question that becomes the turning point in a conversation.

"Is there a special occasion that takes you back?"

Should I tell her? What could I say without telling it all? In truth, I suppose I wanted to talk. Some pain is too hard to hold alone.

So, I said, "We're going to say goodbye to our"—I struggled to find the right words—"to our mother of childhood."

Seeing her puzzled expression, I pushed forward. "She was like our mother. She took care of us. That's not exactly true. She was our mother, but not our biological mother."

"What do you mean by goodbye? Did she—" She could not say that cold word.

"No, she's still living. It's that she won't remember us much longer. We want to say goodbye while she still has some memory left. My brother has questions that he's never asked her—about our history."

"Oh, she has Alzheimer's?"

"Yes. I noticed it when she visited me two years ago. I took her to Disneyland, and she got lost coming out of the bathroom; she didn't recognize me. And she would stare at handicapped people, like children do. She was never like that. She brought us up to be respectful and polite and tolerant." My voice broke and I swallowed the tears that fought to surface.

"How old is she?" the stewardess asked. By now, I had learned her name was Angie. I realized her question was meant to help me gain perspective, but instead I thought, *How can someone be old when she is ageless?*

"She's in her eighties, but she's not old; she's just losing her memory." I could visualize her lively walk and her bright, eager enthusiasm when she saw "her children."

Angie patted my arm and said with kindness, "It's a sad thing to see."

Although her words were true, they felt trite and so insignificant for someone so unique. I wanted her to understand.

"You should have known her. She was a tower, a lighthouse in a storm for hundreds of children. She could make miracles happen. You'd never forget her if you met her," I explained.

"Hundreds of children?" Angie asked with wide eyes.

"Yes, she ran an orphanage. There were over one hundred of us when my brother and I were there. And more before us, and more after we left. Yes, hundreds."

"Where was this place?" she asked, expressing a deepening interest.

"In Eastern Kentucky," I told her.

"You said that she visited you two years ago? What was her name?

"Naomi."

Angie let out a long breath, followed by a quiet laugh. "You're not going to believe this, but I'm sure that I sat with your mother two years ago on her way back from the visit with you. She told me about the orphanage she ran. She was so proud of you. She called you 'one of my girls.' And it is true what you say. She is a woman one could never forget. So many times, I've thought about her and her story."

She paused in reverent silence. Then she said, "There's something I want to tell you about how she influenced me. You see, for years my husband and I tried to have a child. Both of us were reluctant to adopt. But after I met Miss Naomi, I changed my mind—and my heart."

"Did you?" I asked.

"Oh, yes, we have the most delightful little girl. Where does Naomi live?"

I explained how she had recently moved into a memory care facility, a home for retired missionaries in upstate New York.

"Will you tell her something for me?" Angie asked. "Even if she doesn't remember me, tell her Angie remembers her and I will always be thankful for the time I sat with her on the airplane on the way to New York."

My brother and I arrived in time to be able to hear Naomi say once more the words she said to all her children, "You are so special." But her memory was ragged and full of holes. We soon realized that the histories she told about us were jumbled and unreliable.

My brother shook his head sadly after we left. "Sis, I came too late. Now I'll never know the truth of how I came to her. For so many years, I was afraid to know. Now, when I have the courage to look at my beginnings, I'll never know the truth because I never asked."

I reached for his hand and said, "Truth is as ephemeral as memory. But this truth is lasting: we were lucky." He turned and gave me his best smile and a wink.

One truth I took from this journey is this: a casual conversation can take us closer than six degrees of separation.

For Naomi, who passed away in 2006, I wrote the following poem:

Mother Mine

I heard today that you had died
(A cold harsh word); I did not cry.
There was a time when I'd been desolate
And lost without your soft comfort.
Childhood nights of confusing fright,
You calmed and made the world seem right.
And I asked God to take me first, for
Alone I could not face the worst.
      Forever, mother mine!

Youth passed and God had other schemes,
So cruel I lost the voice to scream.
He took your mind before your soul.
All dignity from you he stole.
Then I prayed that you would die.
When No One heard, I dropped the lie
That God protects his followers
And oversees the fall of sparrows.
      Forgive me, mother mine.

Fifteen empty years you lingered
Not knowing names or words you heard,
Unable to walk a wooded lane,
Or read from your God's book again.
I returned before all's erased
In a final show you touched my face.
With all tears spent, I said goodbye,
That's why today I do not cry.
      Farewell, mother mine.

CHAPTER 18

The Mystery of the Missing Money

DAD CAME OUT OF the bedroom waving a stack of one-hundred-dollar bills and commanded me to take him to the bank.

Eyeing what turned out to be ten thousand dollars, I asked, "What on earth are you doing with so much cash in the house?"

He scoffed and said, "Oh, this is nothing! I have dozens more like this hidden, and no one," and he emphatically repeated, "*no one* knows where it is."

That occurrence followed a conversation a few weeks earlier when he bragged about how much wealth he had, adding in a gleeful voice, "I have money no one knows about," trying to titillate my curiosity.

Instead, I responded with, "Dad, if you don't want a stranger to find it, maybe you should leave a note in your trust. Then your executor"—which was me, but I didn't add that—

"could locate it after you're gone. You don't want it to fall into the wrong hands, do you?" I asked.

He eyed me warily and said, "No one comes between me and my money. Even death."

He was ninety-three, and I had begun to worry about his judgment. Recently, he had started taking calls from telemarketers, but first they had to listen to a forty-five-minute story of how he grew up dirt poor in the coal mining hollows of Appalachia and rose to become vice president of a division in one of America's top corporations, after which he'd boast about the money he had amassed. After one caller finally was able to explain that he was offering Dad an opportunity to purchase homeowner's insurance, Dad told the agent outright, "Young man, I don't need insurance. I could build five houses if this one burned down. I self-insure, because I can."

I'd gesture with a slicing motion across my throat, trying to urge him to cut off the conversation when he came close to giving his bank account number to prove his claim. What on earth was he telling them when I wasn't there to hear?

To explain about this obsession he had with money, I need to back up a bit. He grew up in the Great Depression of the thirties, and his self-worth was soundly anchored to the amount in his bank account and a determination to never be poor again. Although he had considerable means, he lived as if he had nothing. He never turned on lights and sat for hours in the dark before bedtime. He refused to turn on the air conditioner on sweltering days or the heat during bitter cold nights. To avoid paying a renewal fee, he sold his car when the time came to reregister it. Then he complained that he didn't have transportation and insisted that I take him grocery shopping; this meant going to five or six different markets where the price of an item might be two cents less. His secluded life revolved around waiting for his monthly bank statement. Finding even a one-cent difference between his accounting and the bank's required a visit to Kristine, his banker. Patiently she'd review every item with him and then sat attentively while he repeated his life story, which started with his birth, described the first fish he ever caught, and summarized every job he'd ever held.

Although his judgment was slipping, he didn't qualify for conservatorship. He could still manage his finances, and although I fixed most of his meals, he knew his way around the kitchen enough not to starve.

After a fall that caused multiple broken bones in his hip, he was hospitalized. At the hospital, I made one last attempt to ask about the money he had hidden.

"You'll never find it," he said. After a pause, he added, "Well, you might, if you dig deep enough."

I had my doubts about his claims. Once, years earlier, he told me about an old man back in the Appalachian hills who upon his deathbed told neighbors he'd buried money near a dogwood tree in his backyard. Dad chuckled with delight as he recounted how neighbors would sneak in after dark to dig in the earth. "They tore up that yard and didn't find a darn nickel."

Dad died from his broken hip injury. I thought I should try at least to find the money before the house was sold. In the past, I'd seen him pay with cash for repairs and new appliances. I could hear him moving about the master bedroom, and then he'd come out with cash, usually a few dollars short, and persuade the servicemen to take the amount as a discount for paying "with real money." They'd usually agree. After they left, he'd laugh at them for being suckers.

So, I started my search in the master bedroom. I looked in his clothes, in drawers, under drawers, in pockets, in the bed posts, under the mattress, in the seams of curtains, behind the toilet, and through the linens. I checked the pantry and freezer. I searched every room and followed all the suggestions that came from friends whose elderly parents had stashed money in strange places. I even looked outside for evidence of his having buried it in the ground. Nothing.

Then again, I wasn't the only one he had told about the hidden money. I'd come to suspect that others might have looked for it while I stayed with Dad in the hospital. Had they found it before I went on my search?

I didn't suspect the Mormons or the Seventh Day Adventists who dropped by. They'd get no further than the front door, as he'd steer them to chairs on the porch and invite them to "visit a spell." The old atheist would listen to their dogmas, then absent diplomacy would start to laugh. "You really can't believe that story. That's the most ridiculous thing I've ever heard. Why, science fiction is more believable. At least they have enough sense to call it fiction." The missionaries eventually gave up on saving his soul and stopped coming around.

But I had four probable suspects: a female acquaintance, Angela, who began to visit regularly, especially on the days when I wasn't there; a caregiver who came two days a week when I couldn't be there with Dad; the painter whom I left on his own to paint sections of Dad's house before his anticipated return home; and the person I arranged to auction his belongings.

Strangely, toward the end, Dad developed contradictions within his cheap nature. He refused to buy new shoes or a new pair of pants when holes appeared, but he gave Angela $1,500 for an airline ticket to visit an ailing aunt in Hawaii. Of course, he could give his money to anyone he wanted, but I thought I should speak to her since I didn't believe the sob stories she told.

"Angela," I said, "you know I just read an article about a woman who manipulated an old fellow out of money. The family brought charges and she ended up in prison."

I didn't hear of any further gifts to Angela after that conversation, but I did learn that she knew where the key to the house was hidden. One day after returning to my father's house after visiting the hospital, I noticed that things were not exactly as I had left them. Someone had entered—someone who had access to a key.

The caregiver also had a key—and tales of woe. She needed surgery on her nose. Indeed, Dad told her, it would definitely improve her appearance. He gave her $3,000, and it wasn't a loan. After the agency learned of this, they stopped sending her.

I hired the painter who had worked at my house in the past. The walls in the master bedroom, walk-in closet, and bath of Dad's house needed a fresh coat of paint after years of no sunlight or fresh air. I paid him his estimated cost and left him on his own to do the job. He moved furniture to the center of the room and prepped the areas. He did an excellent job, but the day after he finished the job he disappeared. I left phone messages for him, but he never returned my calls. I had no way of finding him. Eventually his number was disconnected.

Finally, there was the agent who organized and cleaned and made things ready for an estate sale. I shouldn't have told her that if she came across a large sum of money in sorting through everything, I'd give her a reward. No reward became necessary.

The house sold in a short time to a nice family with three young children. They planned considerable upgrades. The house needed work as it had been neglected for the last ten years of my father's life. "You'll have enough from the estate to take care of what needs doing," he said.

Years passed and my preoccupation with what might have happened to the unaccounted-for money faded. In the beginning, my emotions bounced from anger to confusion to amusement. I pictured all sorts of scenarios about how the money was being spent. I gradually came to believe that the person finding it needed it more than I did, and since my dad had been so penurious all his life, this was his late payment to charity. I was financially secure enough to meet the necessities of life with some left over for indulgences.

I had forgotten about the entire affair until I received an unsigned letter from an unknown source. It read as follows:

> I hope this letter reaches you and finds you in good health. I want to confess my awful injustice to you. It has been eating away at my conscience for many years. I always intended to repay you for the money I stole from your father's house. Now that I am at the end of my life, I don't have it. I took it because it gave me the chance to move and I got a good job paying good wages. I thought of the money as a loan and intended to return it to you. But

I lost the job shortly after. Things didn't work out like I planned. The details aren't necessary. Completing the twelve steps in AA taught me the value of atonement. That's why I want to repay you. I know you think I should be in jail. And I think that sometimes, too, but nature held the trump card. I am near the end. I don't know how much longer I have to live. But until I go, I'd like to pay some of it back to you. Please accept the ten-dollar money order. I will send you one each month until I pass on. I wish it was more, but it's all I can afford out of my disability check. I hope you don't hate me for I have very fond memories of you. All my best wishes.

For crying out loud, who could the letter possibly be from? For a long time, I thought it was the painter when I learned he had bought a spacious home overlooking the ocean. But someone who knew him told me that he had inherited a fortune from his father-in-law. That led me to think it was Angela. I ruined a vacation in Hawaii after shopping in a pricy boutique that she owned. I spent my entire week trying to find out how she had financed the store, only to learn at the end of the vacation that a lover had paid for it. The caregiver could be the culprit. I couldn't track her down because her name changed when she married. By coincidence, I ran into her at a beauty shop in the local area. She brought her client in to have her hair done. Still working as a caregiver, she was probably still working her customers with hard-luck stories.

The estate agent still worked in town, and her circumstances hadn't changed. I doubted that she had found the money.

So, had I overlooked someone?

I waited for the next money order, hoping I could tell from the stamp where it was mailed from. But the envelopes never offered a clue. After a few payments, the money stopped coming.

Some years later, I decided to organize my garage and hired a contractor to install cabinets to store all the junk I'd accumulated. Sorting through what to keep and what to toss, I came across the old army trunk that contained Dad's life history. There were photo albums, old trust papers, bank statements, and miscellaneous items. The trunk definitely must go. The lining had begun to rip and rust was developing on the hinges. Dad had the trunk with him during World War II, and it had followed him the rest of his life. I caressed the torn lining and my hand felt something lumpy. *Must be mold growing or it's rippling from age*, I thought. Then I pulled the lining back as it was already torn. I gasped in shock.

Taped to the back of the lid, so compactly that they formed a solid wall, were plastic sandwich bags filled with one-hundred-dollar bills. I'd gone through this trunk numerous times and never found an iota of evidence that something could be hidden there.

After I recovered from my shock, questions began to surface. *Who, then, was sending me money? How much had the thief taken? How much more had Dad squirreled away?* He had left plenty to see me through my final years. And, finally, the biggest question, *How had he managed to accumulate so much?* I knew his monthly income from his saved payroll receipts, and it didn't account for his wealth. The bigger mystery may be more about the man than about his money. But I doubt I will ever have the answers; his life's book is closed, leaving behind no clues.

CHAPTER 19

A Small Act

RECENTLY I'VE BEEN THINKING about how small actions bring about unexpected results—as if an act could be guided by an awareness outside of one's realm of understanding. What unfolded after a small act of my own left me wondering if a mystical force had a hand in the matter.

On a perfectly ordinary day, the phone rang. "Hello," came the warm greeting. My tongue-tied silence forced the caller to say, "It's Sam," which was followed by a familiar laugh, the voice of a friend I had not seen for twenty years.

I stammered, "Where are you?"

"Not far from you. I just called to say hello and to say goodbye."

In the past I would have construed these words to mean he was on his way to another adventure for he was a man who traveled the world. But I knew before he told me that he meant something vastly different.

"You're dying," I whispered.

"Yes," he said without emotion.

"Please, come see us. Let's say goodbye in person. Don't do this alone," I pleaded, knowing his hermitlike tendencies.

My friend Sam chose the life of a solitary wanderer. I met him when I was a young student in college. He awakened in me an appreciation of ancient history, he tried to teach me to read stock charts, and he was skeptical about most things, especially if it involved politics. He'd often quote Santayana: "Skepticism is the chastity of the intellect, it is shameful to surrender it too soon or to the first comer." Perhaps he lived alone because he adhered to certain unconventional beliefs about life and marriage. Living the life of a gypsy, he felt completely at home in the numerous countries in which he resided, claiming no allegiance to any. When I knew him, he read several international newspapers a day and referred to himself as a citizen of the world. He had invested wisely so that "I can live the life of a comfortable hobo." He was a private and elusive man who never talked about his past or his present life. My private fantasy was that he worked for the CIA. Over the span of forty years, he appeared and disappeared in my life like a migrating bird. His last visit had been nearly twenty years earlier. During that visit I did a small thing, unexplainable to myself at the time, that brought about a memorable outcome.

On that visit, he made a telephone call to a sister I didn't know he had. I came into the study at the end of the conversation to witness frustration and resignation on his face. "I've given up," he sighed. "Nancy's making a real mistake by marrying this man." And with that he tossed a scrap of paper into the trash. He stayed several days and then vanished. As I was taking out the trash a few days later, my eyes fell on the discarded note with the name Nancy and a phone number.

I retrieved it from the trash and tucked it into the bottom of my jewelry box.

Years later, while packing and disposing of nonessentials for the move to my current home, I came across the note. I called the phone number scribbled on it. I introduced myself to Nancy as Sam's longtime friend. "When you hear from him, tell him I've moved to north San Diego County."

She replied, "I don't expect to hear from him. I'm sure he's dead. There's been too many years of silence."

In my heart I felt she was wrong. I almost tossed out the scrap of paper, but after a brief hesitation, I placed it back into the jewelry box. Then I forgot about it.

Now he had come to say a final goodbye. The cancer and the years had nibbled away at his youthful physique. His bent posture and slow movements were a change from the lithe athlete he'd been. Throughout the visit, we talked of many things: of politics, of memories, and of death. Just before he left, he commented offhandedly, "I've been thinking of looking up my sister. She remarried and I can't remember her husband's last name." He shrugged and then added, "Oh, maybe it's not worth the effort. We were never that close." He paused and said without regret, "I've only got a few weeks left."

"Wait," I said, "I'll be right back!" I ran to locate my jewelry box and found the small note on which he had written his sister's phone number. I told him how close I'd come to throwing it out, but something stopped me. He tucked the worn piece of paper into his pocket and said with a smile, "Maybe I'll call her, maybe not." And he left.

A few days later I answered the phone to hear Sam's broken voice. "You don't know what a gift you've given me." Although he was a man who never expressed emotion, his voice choked as he told me of the reunion with his sister. Such a small act as saving a piece of paper brought about a closure I would never have imagined. I allow myself to believe that my nomadic friend finally found a home and a place to die where he would not be alone.

In a way, I hope there is some *thing* that guides our small actions. Some of my friends believe in angels, but I'm more inclined to embrace Aristotle's concept of intuitive wisdom. I only wish I had more of it.

In honor of my friend's life and leaving, I wrote these words:

Back to the Light

I didn't think that death would come
    With a dark song and kind eyes,
Begging my pardon for coming
    So late to say goodbye.
Weeks, you said, I've only weeks left.
    Where will you go, I asked?
And you said, Back to my origin,
    The far side of 14 billion years—
Back to the Light.

I remembered an afternoon, years past, when we
    Lingered in my garden. I could not escape
The sparks of light that streamed from your eyes
    Falling like shards of a broken vessel.
Believing the sun played tricks with my vision,
    I moved my position, but the light
Grew until it enclosed us in a sphere—
    Until I looked away in fear.

Now I understand. I saw your beginning and
    Your end—your cosmic signature.
One day when it comes my night tc scatter across
    The sky, my light will know your light,
    And old friends will reunite.

CHAPTER 20

The Ring

EXHAUSTED AND BRAIN WEARY from a long day of listening to dry lectures, I dropped into a chair and was prepared to spend the dinner in silence. Almost immediately I noticed the ring on the hand of the man sitting next to me. The ring itself was an ordinary gold band, but the large stone embedded in it was extraordinary. At first it appeared apple green, but when I looked again, it had turned to shades of emerald green with streaks of daffodil yellow and magenta. I thought the refraction of light or the movement of his hand caused the colors to change. My eyes kept returning to the ring; I was fascinated by it. The changing combination of its shades reminded me of the northern lights I'd seen in the Alaskan sky. I began to wonder if it was alive.

Finally, I surrendered to curiosity and asked, "What stone is that?"

"I don't know. It was a gift." I noted the lyrical music of his accent and guessed he was from India. His polite but inattentive response told me that the man too may have been weary and wanted privacy.

Hundreds of us were seated in a cavernous dining room, ten per table, waiting for dinner and the final speaker of the day. Anyone who has been to a psychiatric conference knows that most of the lectures are about as boring as standing in line at a supermarket. We endure it because it is required to renew our license. I had gone with the attitude of fulfilling a professional obligation. Little did I expect to hear something out of the ordinary.

Stealing a look at the ring owner and glancing at his name tag, I read, "Sanjay Dalal, MD."

Another clue that he was from India! Memories of my visits to that country flooded my mind. How vividly I recalled the gritty taste and the pink glow of sunrise, the magical light that bathed the land in an otherworldly aura—bathed it with beauty and with bacteria. The pungent smells of cow dung, urine, and rich aromatic spices intermingled. The India that settled in my lungs and that I spit up for three months after I left. The India of temples and holy rituals. I blushed as I recalled the oven-hot night when I sat on the balcony of a small, elegant hotel overlooking the ghats and watched in awe the thousands who came to bathe in the holy waters. Suddenly I felt a sharp sting on my stomach. *Oh, God, a scorpion. I'm going to die in India.* I let out a scream and leaped to my feet, tearing off my blouse at the same time and flinging it across the floor. It turned out not to be a scorpion, but only a bee. My startled Indian host rushed to the kitchen to find a raw potato and calmly applied it to the injured area. It was metaphor for India! Just when you think you've found it, you get stung, making you realize you know nothing of India.

"Where do you live?" I asked Dr. Dalal.

"Milwaukee."

"And before there? I thought I detected an Indian accent."

"I grew up in Madras. Have you been to India?" he asked politely.

"Only to the golden triangle region." He nodded, knowing I spoke of Delhi, Agra, Jaipur, Jodhpur, and the golden city of Jaisalmer in the heart of the Great Indian Desert.

Maybe it was my smile or something he heard in my voice, but he seemed to know that I had been stung by India. "What did you like most about India?" he asked in a friendly voice.

"Oh, the temples. The exotic gods."

"Which was your favorite god?"

"Ganesh, the elephant. Elephants are intelligent and have long memories. Sometimes I feel like the western God has forgotten about man."

The door opened and we began a friendly conversation, starting with the differences in eastern and western religions and the tensions within religions as they seek to find balance between a personal god and impersonal one. We spoke of politics, the recent election, our work, and family. I learned that he was married and had a young daughter and that he practiced psychiatry in a public mental health clinic. His kind manner and balanced outlook drew me to him. I even confessed my worry about the present chaos in the world.

He replied calmly, "Life is like a flowing river. It's the whirl and flux that bring change. And sometimes its force causes destruction. Nothing is permanent."

He must have noticed my continued interest in the ring, for suddenly he said, "I will tell you about the ring. Do you know of Sai Baba?"

"No. Is he a guru?"

"He is a spiritual leader. He's well known for his charitable works, for building hospitals and schools. He doesn't ask for any donations, but people give willingly. If he says, 'This village needs a school for the children,' before long it is built. That is the kind of man he is.

"My wife has admired him for many years. Last year we returned to India on holiday and she heard he would be speaking nearby. I'd never been deeply religious, but I agreed to go with her. There were thousands at the gathering. After he finished speaking, he came down to mingle among us. We were surprised when he stopped directly in front of us, and gesturing to me, asked, 'You, your wife, and little girl, would you come and spend time with me this afternoon?' I saw my wife's face flush with joy."

"What an honor that he chose you. What was he like?"

"Amazing. You know, speaking with him felt so natural. We spoke of simple things, then deeper things, things of the heart. It was like talking to a close friend."

I hoped that he'd tell me that Sai Baba had revealed a secret truth, something that would make sense of mankind's follies, something that would give me hope for humanity. Instead he told of an astonishing happening.

"We spoke for several hours. Just as we were getting ready to leave, Sai Baba asked if I'd accept a gift. I felt humbled. Then he reached up and out of the air he produced this ring. He handed it to me. I slipped it on my finger, and it fit perfectly."

Magic, I thought to myself. *A timeless trick.*

"The ring was clear, like crystal or unclouded glass. Then Sai Baba asked for it back, saying it wasn't quite right for me. I handed it back to him. He then breathed on the ring three times and handed it back to me. This is the color that it turned," he said, stretching out his hand to display the ring. "It has stayed the same since he breathed on it."

I felt goose bumps rise along my arms. We both sat in silence, gazing at the ring. I struggled with my doubt.

"It was not magic," he said. "I watched carefully. I would not have believed had I not seen it with my own eyes. What I tell you is the truth."

"Did he say why he gave it to you?" I asked.

"Yes. For inner peace."

My hand involuntarily moved toward the ring and I touched it lightly. "I could use a little of that myself."

I half expected that a tidal wave would wash over me, flooding me with enlightenment, freeing me from personal demons, or elevating me to a state of bliss. But I felt nothing.

"Do you know the mineral content of the stone?"

"That's the strange thing. I've taken it to several highly regarded gemologists, and none of them know what it is. They can't identify it."

At that moment, the lights in the dining room dimmed and our speaker, who was to illuminate us on "Coexisting Anxiety and Depression" was introduced.

The conference has dimmed in my mind as well, but not the story of the ring. I have thought about it often. Could what the doctor told about the ring be true? Did it really happen as he reported?

Although no epiphany occurred, and no sudden profound insight into life's meaning emerged when I touched the ring, I have discovered that it did have the power to alter energy. You see, now when I become worked up over world affairs or minutiae, the colors of the ring materialize in my mind's eye. I hear the doctor's words, "Life is like a flowing river" and I let that river carry me to a place of inner peace. This transformation is greater than the materialization of matter from thin air, or so it seems to me.

CHAPTER 21

Silhouettes

FOR TWENTY-FIVE YEARS, I owned a vacation home on an island just across the Canadian border. The house sits on a hill overlooking a panoramic view of the Georgia Strait, where ferries glide in the reflection of snowcapped mountains. It is on one of the most pristine and beautiful of the Gulf Islands. Nearly half of the island is preserved parkland. Because it sits in the lee of the Olympic mountain range, the island's annual rainfall is about thirty inches, barely enough to meet the water needs year-round.

My husband and I found the island after we chartered a boat out of Anacortes, Washington, and motored through the San Juan Islands and then into Canadian waters. Because of the wild tides and currents, we chartered a power boat rather than a sailboat. On our first journey, we invited a friend who serenaded us with the music of his flute at sunrise and sunset. As we made our way from island to island, we observed blue herons, Canada geese, and cormorants in flight. One afternoon, a sudden happy surprise greeted us: we idled the boat to behold a pod of orcas surround us, breeching, rolling, splashing, and laughing before the creatures moved on.

Maybe it was the music of the flute or the magic of the orcas, or the breathtaking beauty of arbutus, fir, and cypress that caused me to undergo a mystical experience. While taking a solitary stroll along the cliffs of one of the islands, I heard a voice and felt a hand on my shoulder. The voice said, "Girl, you've come home." Then I knew I had to have a piece of this land.

By the next summer, we owned six acres of nirvana. The island brought serenity and lunacy and a metaphor I chose for my life. This story is about claiming my metaphor.

Upon our arrival with plans to spend the summer, the island was abuzz with the exciting news that a cougar had been spotted. Twelve goats had been killed on the Campbells' farm. The village newspaper published conflicting views about whether a cougar could swim all the way from the mainland. Children on the island wrote letters to the local paper saying they were sure their parents would never allow a cougar to live among them and would have already killed it. Others claimed the goats had been killed by passing sailors who jumped ship in the strait while waiting for clearance into the Port of Vancouver, asserting they came to hunt while waiting for the longshoremen's strike to be settled. But a credible voice from the fire department reported that in fact a cougar had been spotted by Mr. deVane.

Cougars! I was determined that this animal would not stop my planned three-mile hike to the plateau of the island's two-thousand-foot-high mountain. The *Los Angeles Times* called it one of the most beautiful views in the world. From there, one could walk along cliffs where eagles soared below, and islands lay scattered like jewels from an unstrung necklace. From this heavenly height, I would view the sunset and look across the water all the way to the city of Victoria. Leaving the house after dinner, I told my husband, "If I'm not back in an hour and a half, bring the car and pick me up." I was thinking about cougars coming out after dark.

Why had I said I'd be back in an hour and half? That meant I'd have to hike the three miles and then back down without a break to enjoy the view.

Summer days are long in this part of the world, with sunset arriving around nine-thirty. The warm evening air lured me into daydreaming. I walked past the lumber mill, turning left just before the lake reservoir that catches our rainwater for drinking, and began the long, steep climb to the top. The unpaved road wound through pristine forests flanked with purple foxgloves, which bowed as I passed. I strolled like a woman in love, for I was in love with my island. Up I climbed with vigor and determination. As my legs began to protest, I thought, *I don't remember it being this far when I drove it.* But I knew I was on the right road since there is only one road to the top. So, I continued.

The thick forest blocked the sunlight and the road became dark and forbidding. Screeching sounds echoed from the treetops and rustling deep within the forest aroused my imagination. I began to worry about cougars and bobcats and ocelots and lions. Walking faster until my heart pounded so loud that I thought it would explode, I turned the corner and saw the communication tower looming ahead: *The Top.* I had arrived. But standing between me and my desired destination, stood a very large animal with a great mane and a small swishing tail.

Omigod! A lion! No—the cougar. I turned and ran back down the hill as fast as my exhausted legs could carry me, all the while sizing up every tree that I passed, searching for one to climb before the cougar made its final hungry leap for me. *But don't cats climb trees?* I asked myself. As I was running, I was thinking, *That thing didn't look like a cougar. Does the male cougar have a great mane like a lion?* I wasn't going to take a chance. What could it be? In my delirious condition, I became certain it was a lion.

Rounding a corner, I saw our red Tracker approach. My husband! I flagged him down, jumped inside, and pointed up the road. "A lion!" I gulped, out of breath.

He laughed, "There's no lions in this part of the world."

"Then it's the cougar. With a mane. I'll prove it. Take me to the top." I knew I must go back and face whatever monster waited or I'd never take this beautiful walk again.

I sat forward, gripping the dash, growing more vigilant as we neared the top. When we turned the last curve, there stood the same large, menacing animal. The setting sun behind him magnified his size. We approached slowly, for the sun was blinding our view. I held my breath, expecting to see the cougar. Then, at the same moment, both of us broke into laughter. Instead of a cougar or a lion, standing there was Mr. Campbell's old billy goat, his matted mane waving in the breeze. He appeared stoic and unimpressed as the vehicle made its way toward him. Slowly he turned and walked away.

I laughed until tears ran down my cheeks. How easy it is to misinterpret facts in the face of fear—to see danger when something harmless is in front of us. This experience became my chosen metaphor for life: with every crisis I ask, "Is this a lion or is it Mr. Campbell's billy goat?"

Epilogue

IN WRITING THESE STORIES, I had no agenda; I was not trying to teach or lay out a way to be or pontificate. The bigger question is not why I wrote these stories but why humans tell stories. Storytelling is embedded in our nature and important in transmitting our culture. When we look back to our earliest beginnings, we see that stories were told by our ancient ancestors around a bonfire, later in epic poems or through mythological tales, and much later in novel form. I believe the reason for this persistent activity is to search for who we are.

As I stepped away and took a telescopic look at the collection of stories I wrote, I saw how ordinarily human I was. I found a person with clashing contradictions. I could be adamant about something yet wrong; naïve, even stupidly so, yet also skeptical; I could be blindly courageous and terrified; I could be determined, yet doubtful. I could spout both idealism and disillusionment. I could be both compassionate and unfeeling.

As humans, we are a mixture of conflicting inconsistencies, and I believe one indication of good mental health is the ability to balance them. I think I manage this struggle through forgiving myself for my imperfections and continuing the search for understanding. Stories often help us find a way to do just that.

I am fortunate to have been blessed with an abundance of curiosity. It has spared me from boredom and also allowed me to be open to new ideas and to take risks. It has been my ally through challenging times.

Now with this project complete, I had hoped that COVID-19 would have been downgraded to a disease no more threatenig than a common cold. However, the virus had other plans and mutated, causing once again worldwide panic. Now I wait on pins and needles for a vaccination that will give me back some degree of freedom. And I wish, like everyone else, for our lives to return to normal. Perhaps with additional time for reflection, I may surprise myself with more stories to tell, for to a storyteller, an everyday, common occurrence can become a narrative.

Acknowledgments

I WISH TO GIVE special recognition to the editors at PeopleSpeak, who have worked closely with me on my books. I am deeply appreciative of their professional guidance, attention to detail, and support.

About the Author

Delores "Dee" Wardell, PhD, is the author of *Naomi's Place, The Charm Bracelet,* and *My Sister's Keeper: Maude's Story.* She grew up in a children's home like the one in her novels. She became a clinical psychologist and family therapist, and her professional career included work in the judicial system evaluating families, adults, and children for the court. She also had a private practice. She is retired and enjoys her time traveling, writing, and playing the harp. She lives in North San Diego County, California. For more information, visit deloreswardell.com.

www.ingramcontent.com/pod-product-compliance
Lightning Source LLC
Chambersburg PA
CBHW020327110726
47898CB00003B/778